Data Extraction with .NET and C#: Zero to Hero in Web Scraping

Copyright Page

© 2025 by Ali Jafari
All rights reserved.

No part of this book may be reproduced, stored in a retrieval system, or transmitted in any form or by any means, electronic, mechanical, photocopying, recording, or otherwise, without prior written permission from the publisher, except for the use of brief quotations in a review.

Published by Self Publishing | Amazon Kindle Direct Publishing
USA / Germany

First Edition: 2025
ISBN: 9798305118919

Imprint: Independently published

Cover Design: KDP
Printed On Demand in Countries

alijafarixcs@gmail.com

linkedin.com/in/ali-jafari-a08386157

Edit: Shohreh Jafari : sh.jafari.en@gmail.com

Preface

In today's data-driven world, the ability to gather information from the internet has become an essential skill. Web scraping allows us to collect vast amounts of data efficiently and can be a game-changer for businesses, researchers, and developers. This book is designed to guide you through the process of web scraping using .NET and C#, two powerful tools that are both accessible and versatile.

Whether you're a beginner or an experienced developer, you'll find step-by-step instructions, real-world examples, and tips to help you master the art of web scraping. From understanding the fundamentals of data extraction to advanced techniques for handling complex websites, this guide will equip you with everything you need to get started—and succeed.

My goal with this book is not only to teach you how to scrape data but also to inspire confidence in your ability to solve real-world problems using C# and .NET. I hope you find this guide useful, practical, and enjoyable as you embark on your journey of becoming a proficient web scraper.

Thank you for choosing this book, and I wish you success as you move from a novice to a web scraping pro.

Special Thanks

I would like to take a moment to express my sincere gratitude to everyone who supported me throughout this journey. Special thanks to my mentors, colleagues, and friends, whose guidance and encouragement helped shape this project. A big thank you to my family for their unwavering support and understanding during the long hours spent writing this book.

A heartfelt thank you to the .NET and C# communities. Your contributions, knowledge-sharing, and passion for programming continue to inspire me daily.

Finally, I would like to extend my deepest appreciation to you, the reader. Without your interest in learning and improving your skills, this book would not have been possible. I hope it serves you well on your journey to mastering web scraping and data collection.

Who This Book Is For

This book is designed for a wide range of readers, from absolute beginners to experienced developers looking to expand their skill set in web scraping using .NET and C#. Whether you are:

1. **A Beginner Programmer**
   If you're new to programming, especially with C# or .NET, this book provides clear, step-by-step explanations to help you get up to speed with the core concepts of web scraping and data collection. You'll be guided through each topic with practical examples to ensure you gain both knowledge and hands-on experience.

2. **An Aspiring Web Scraping Developer**
   If you're someone looking to learn how to gather data from the internet efficiently, this book is perfect for you. We'll cover the techniques and best practices to help you collect and process data from websites, no matter the complexity.

3. **A C# Developer Seeking to Expand Your Skillset**
   If you're already familiar with C# and .NET but want to enhance your expertise by diving into web scraping, this book is a great fit. You'll learn how to apply your existing knowledge in a new context while mastering data extraction techniques.

4. **A Data Enthusiast or Researcher**
   If you're in research or data-driven fields, web scraping is a valuable tool to automate the collection of data from various online sources. This book will teach you how to use C# and .NET to access and manipulate data from websites effectively.

5. **A Professional Looking to Build Real-World Projects**
   Whether you're working in business intelligence, data science, or any field that requires large-scale data collection, this book provides you with the skills and know-how to automate your data gathering process, making you more productive and efficient.

This book will guide you through both simple and complex scraping tasks, making it suitable for learners at all levels of experience.

Contents

Data Extraction with .NET and C#: Zero to Hero in Web Scraping 1
    Copyright Page 2
    Preface 3
    Special Thanks 3
    Who This Book Is For 3
Contents 4
Chapter 1: Treasure in the **Internet** 9
    1.1 Dive into the Ocean of Data: Unlocking the Secrets of the Internet 9
    1.2 The Value of Web Scraping: Unlocking Business Potential 10
    1.2.1 What is Web Scraping? 10
    1.2.2 Key Use Cases 11
    1.2.3 Legal and Ethical Considerations 11
    1.3 Real-World Examples: Web Scraping in Action 12
    1.4 Uncovering Hidden Opportunities: The Power of Web Scraping 12
Chapter 2: Getting Started with C# 13
    2.1 What is .NET and C#? 14
    2.2 Installing Visual Studio and Setting Up the Environment 14

2.3 Basic C# Syntax and Concepts 15
2.4 Introduction to Libraries and NuGet Packages 18
2.5 Object-Oriented Programming (OOP) in C# 20
1. Classes and Objects: 22
2. Inheritance: 25
3. Polymorphism: 26
4. Encapsulation: 28
5. Abstraction: 29

Chapter 3: HTTP, the Protocol of Internet 31
3.1 Understanding HTTP and HTML 31
How the Web Works: HTTP and HTTPS Protocols 31
HTTP Request and Response 32
The HTTP Request-Response Lifecycle 32
HTTPS (Hypertext Transfer Protocol Secure): 32
SSL/TLS Encryption: 32
Trust and Authentication: 32
Why HTTPS is Important 32
3.2 HTML: The Language of Web Pages 33
HTML 33
Basic Structure of HTML 33
Basics of DOM (Document Object Model) 35
Manipulating DOM Elements: You 36
3.3 Tools for Inspecting and Analyzing Web Pages 36
1. Browser Developer Tools (DevTools): 37
Key Features of DevTools 37
2. Lighthouse 37
3. WebPageTest 37
4. Fiddler 37
5. Chrome Extensions 37
- Wappalyzer 37
- BuiltWith 37

Chapter 4: Core Libraries for Web Scraping in C# 38
4.1 Overview of HttpClient for HTTP Requests 38
4.2 Using HtmlAgilityPack for Parsing HTML 39
4.3 Exploring AngleSharp for Advanced Scraping 41
4.5 Handling Dynamic Content 42

4.6 Best Practices for Web Scraping 43

Conclusion 43

Chapter 5: Building Your First Web Scraper 44

5.1 Fetching Web Pages with HttpClient 45

5.2 Crawling Links from Sitemap and Saving Results 49

Example of Sitemap Structure 53

5.3 Extracting Data with HtmlAgilityPack 54

Introduction to XPath 54

Basic XPath Syntax 54

XPath Axes 55

XPath Functions 55

Using XPath with HtmlAgilityPack 55

Common XPath Expressions 56

Combining XPath Expressions 56

Chapter 6: Advanced Data Extraction Techniques 58

6.1 Introduction to Selenium for Browser Automation in C# 58

6.2 Handling JavaScript-Rendered Content 59

6.3 Interacting with Forms, Buttons, and Dropdowns 60

6.4 Handling Cookies and Sessions 61

6.5 Advanced Crawling with Asynchronous Tasks in C# 62

Chapter Summary 65

Chapter 7. Working with APIs 66

7.1 RESTful APIs and How They Work 66

Steps: 66

Explanation: 68

Running the Code: 68

Steps: 69

Explanation: 71

Running the Client: 72

7.2 Fetching and Parsing API Data in C# 72

7.3 Managing Authentication for APIs 76

7.4 Using Third-Party APIs for Web Scraping 77

7.5 Advanced Topics in API Integration 77

7.6 Troubleshooting and Debugging API Issues 79

Debugging Tools: 79

Logging and Monitoring: 80

Handling API Errors: 80

Code Example by implementing Error Handling and HTTP Error codes: 82

Chapter 8.Data Storage and Export 87

Importance of Saving Data 87

8.1 Saving Data to CSV, JSON, and Databases 87

CSV (Comma-Separated Values) 87

JSON (JavaScript Object Notation) 89

Databases 91

SQL Server 93

SQLite 93

8.3 Using Entity Framework for Data Handling 94

Database-First Approach 94

Code-First Approach 95

CRUD (Create, Read, Update, Delete) 96

2. Read (Get All) 97

3. Read (Get By Id) 97

4. Update 98

5. Delete 98

Chapter 9.Deploying and Automating Your Scraper 99

9.1: Introduction to Deploying and Automating Your Scraper 99

1. Understanding Deployment Needs 100

2. Automation and Scheduling 100

3. Implementing Automation 100

4. Steps to Deploy 105

5. Logging and Monitoring 105

6. Security and Best Practices 105

9.2 Hosting Your ASP.NET Scrapers on Azure or AWS 106

Hosting on Microsoft Azure 106

Hosting on Amazon Web Services (AWS) 107

Choosing Between Azure and AWS 108

Development process for Azure 109

Vision 109

Development environment for ASP.NET Core apps 109

Development workflow for Azure-hosted ASP.NET Core apps 110

References 113

Chapter 10. Azure hosting recommendations for ASP.NET Core web apps 114

7

Web applications 114

Logical processes 120

Data 120

Architecture recommendations 121

Chapter 1: Treasure in the Internet

1.1 Dive into the Ocean of Data: Unlocking the Secrets of the Internet

The internet is a vast, ever-changing landscape where over 4.3 billion people generate a staggering 2.5 quintillion bytes of data every day. With social media platforms, online transactions, IoT devices, and online content creation, the internet is a treasure trove of information waiting to be explored. Social media platforms generate over 500 million tweets, 4.4 million Facebook posts, and 95 million Instagram posts daily. Online transactions exceed 1 billion per day, transforming commerce and enabling unprecedented convenience and efficiency. IoT devices add over 5.5 million new data points every minute, offering insights into personal health, industrial operations, and more. YouTube alone sees over 500 hours of new video content uploaded every minute, enriching the digital ecosystem. The internet is a dynamic, ever-changing entity that's revolutionizing the way we live, work, and interact. It's a repository of information, a platform for communication, and a catalyst for innovation. With the internet, we can access information, connect with people, and share ideas like never before. However, navigating this ocean of data presents significant challenges, including data privacy concerns and information overload. To overcome these challenges, we need advanced data extraction and analysis techniques, such as machine learning and natural language processing. These techniques can help us harness the internet's vast resources and unlock new opportunities for growth and innovation. By leveraging the internet's power, we can drive economic development, improve healthcare, and enhance education. We can also use the internet to promote social justice, protect the environment, and preserve cultural heritage. The internet is a powerful tool that can be used for good or ill, and it's up to us to ensure that it's used responsibly and for the greater good. As we move forward in this digital age, it's essential that we prioritize data privacy, security, and ethics. We must also ensure that the internet is accessible to all, regardless of geographical location or socio-economic status. By working together, we can create a more equitable, just, and prosperous world for all. The internet is a vast ocean of data, and it's up to us to explore it, harness its power, and unlock its secrets. With the right strategies and technologies, we can turn the internet into a powerful tool for positive change. So let's dive into the ocean of data and start exploring its vast possibilities.

1.2 The Value of Web Scraping: Unlocking Business Potential

Web scraping has emerged as a cornerstone of modern data-driven strategies, empowering organizations to extract, analyze, and utilize online data effectively. By leveraging web scraping, businesses can gain valuable insights into consumer behavior, market dynamics, and competitor activity. Web scraping can be used for market research, competitor analysis, business intelligence, and product development. It can help businesses identify new opportunities, optimize their operations, and improve their bottom line. With web scraping, companies can analyze large datasets, identify trends and patterns, and make data-driven decisions. Web scraping is a powerful tool that can be used to drive innovation, improve efficiency, and reduce costs. It can help businesses stay ahead of the competition, anticipate market trends, and adapt to changing consumer behavior. By leveraging web scraping, organizations can unlock new revenue streams, expand their customer base, and improve their brand reputation. Web scraping can also be used to monitor social media conversations, track online reviews, and analyze customer feedback. It can help businesses identify areas for improvement, optimize their customer service, and enhance their overall customer experience. With web scraping, companies can make informed decisions, drive growth, and achieve their strategic objectives. Web scraping is a valuable tool that can be used to drive business success, and it's an essential component of any data-driven strategy. By leveraging web scraping, businesses can gain a competitive edge, improve their operations, and achieve their goals. So why not start web scraping today and unlock the full potential of your business?

1.2.1 What is Web Scraping?

Definition: Web scraping is the automated process of extracting data from websites. Unlike manual copying and pasting, web scraping uses programs to fetch and process the required data efficiently.

How it Works (High-Level):

- Web scraping involves sending HTTP requests to a website to retrieve its HTML content.
- The HTML is parsed to extract specific data points using tools and libraries.
- The extracted data is then structured and saved for further analysis or usage.

Web Scraping vs. Web Crawling/Spidering:

- Web crawling focuses on discovering and indexing web pages, typically for search engines.
- Web scraping extracts specific data from discovered pages.

Types of Web Scraping:

- Parsing HTML/XML: Using libraries like Beautiful Soup or lxml to process static web pages.
- Using APIs: Preferred when websites offer APIs for data access, reducing ethical and technical challenges.
- Headless Browsers: Tools like Selenium or Playwright help scrape dynamic content rendered by JavaScript.

1.2.2 Key Use Cases

- Market Research:
  o Monitoring and comparing prices.
  o Analyzing product reviews and sentiment.
  o Identifying market trends.

- Lead Generation:
  o Collecting contact information (e.g., emails, phone numbers) ethically.
  o Creating targeted marketing lists.

- Competitive Analysis:
  o Tracking competitor pricing and offerings.
  o Monitoring marketing strategies and SEO performance.

- Other Use Cases:
  o Data journalism, academic research, real estate aggregation, and financial analysis.

1.2.3 Legal and Ethical Considerations

- Terms of Service and Robots.txt: Adhere to the rules in a website's robots.txt file and terms of service to respect its data usage policies.
- Rate Limiting and Avoiding Overloading Servers: Implement delays between requests to avoid overwhelming a website's servers.
- Data Privacy and GDPR/CCPA Compliance: Handle personal data responsibly to avoid legal risks associated with privacy violations.
- Copyright and Intellectual Property: Be cautious of using scraped data in ways that might infringe intellectual property rights.

- Best Practices: Follow ethical guidelines, such as avoiding restricted areas and seeking permission when needed.

1.3 Real-World Examples: Web Scraping in Action

Web scraping is being used by businesses and organizations across various industries to drive growth, improve efficiency, and reduce costs. For example, a retail company can use web scraping to track product prices, monitor competitor activity, and optimize their pricing strategy. A market research firm can use web scraping to analyze social media conversations, track online trends, and identify emerging market opportunities. A company can use web scraping to monitor customer reviews, track online feedback, and improve their customer service. Web scraping can also be used to analyze large datasets, identify trends and patterns, and make data-driven decisions. For instance, a business can use web scraping to analyze customer purchase history, identify buying patterns, and develop targeted marketing campaigns. Web scraping can also be used to track online conversations, monitor brand mentions, and measure social media engagement. By leveraging web scraping, businesses can gain valuable insights into consumer behavior, market dynamics, and competitor activity. Web scraping can help companies stay ahead of the competition, anticipate market trends, and adapt to changing consumer behavior. It can also be used to identify new business opportunities, optimize operations, and improve the bottom line. With web scraping, organizations can unlock new revenue streams, expand their customer base, and improve their brand reputation. So why not start web scraping today and drive business success?

1.4 Uncovering Hidden Opportunities: The Power of Web Scraping

Web scraping can be used to uncover hidden opportunities, identify new business ideas, and develop innovative products and services. By analyzing large datasets, identifying trends and patterns, and making data-driven decisions, businesses can gain a competitive edge. Web scraping can help companies anticipate market trends, adapt to changing consumer behavior, and stay ahead of the competition. It can also be used to identify new revenue streams, expand the customer base, and improve the brand reputation. With web scraping, organizations can unlock new opportunities, drive growth, and achieve their strategic objectives. Web scraping can be used to analyze customer feedback, track online reviews, and improve the overall customer experience. It can also be used to monitor social media conversations, track online trends, and measure social media engagement. By leveraging web scraping, businesses can gain valuable insights into consumer behavior, market dynamics, and competitor activity. Web scraping can help companies make informed decisions, drive innovation, and achieve their goals. It's a powerful tool that can be used to drive business success, and it's an essential component of any data-driven strategy. So why not start web scraping today and unlock the full potential of your business? With web scraping, you can uncover hidden opportunities, identify new business ideas, and develop innovative products and services. You can gain a competitive edge, drive growth, and achieve your strategic objectives. So start web scraping today and take your business to the next level!

Chapter 2: Getting Started with C#

2.1 What is .NET and C#?

The .NET Framework and C# are two of the most powerful tools in the world of software development. .NET is a software framework developed by Microsoft, while C# is a modern, object-oriented programming language developed by Microsoft as part of the .NET initiative. The .NET Framework provides a large set of libraries and APIs for building Windows-based applications, including libraries for file I/O, networking, database access, and user interface development.

C# is designed to work seamlessly with the .NET Framework, allowing developers to write efficient, reliable, and scalable code. With its strong typing, garbage collection, and modern language features, C# has become a popular choice for developing a wide range of applications, including Windows desktop and mobile apps, web applications, games, and enterprise software systems.

Key Features of C#:

- Object-Oriented Programming (OOP) Support: C# supports encapsulation, inheritance, and polymorphism, making it easy to write reusable and maintainable code.
- Statically-Typed Language: C# is a statically-typed language, which means that the compiler checks the types of variables at compile time, preventing type-related errors at runtime.
- Garbage Collection: C# has automatic memory management through garbage collection, which reduces the risk of memory leaks and other memory-related issues.
- Multi-Threading Support: C# supports multi-threading, which allows developers to write concurrent systems that can take advantage of multi-core processors.

2.2 Installing Visual Studio and Setting Up the Environment

To get started with C#, you'll need to install Visual Studio, which is the official integrated development environment (IDE) for C# development. Visual Studio provides a comprehensive set of tools for writing, debugging, and testing C# code, including a code editor, a debugger, and a project manager.

Steps to Install Visual Studio and Set Up the Environment:

1. Download the Visual Studio Installer: Visit the official Microsoft website and download the Visual Studio installer.
2. Run the Installer: Run the installer and follow the prompts to select the edition of Visual Studio you want to install.
3. Choose the .NET Desktop Development Workload: Ensure that you select the .NET desktop development workload, which includes the C# compiler and runtime.
4. Install Additional Components: You may also want to install additional components, such as the Windows SDK or the .NET Core framework.
5. Launch Visual Studio: Once the installation is complete, launch Visual Studio and create a new project.

Key Features of Visual Studio:

- Code Editor: Visual Studio has a powerful code editor with syntax highlighting, auto-completion, and code refactoring.
- Debugger: Visual Studio has a built-in debugger that allows you to step through your code, inspect variables, and set breakpoints.
- Project Manager: Visual Studio has a project manager that allows you to create, manage, and build projects.
- Build and Deployment Tools: Visual Studio has build and deployment tools that allow you to create and deploy C# applications.

2.3 Basic C# Syntax and Concepts

C# is a modern, object-oriented programming language that is designed to work with the .NET Framework. The syntax and concepts of C# are based on the C and C++ programming languages, but it has many additional features and improvements that make it a more efficient and effective language for building Windows-based applications.

Basic Syntax Elements:

- Variables: Variables are used to store and manipulate data. In C#, you can declare variables using the var keyword or by specifying the data type explicitly.
- Data Types: C# has a rich set of data types, including integers, floating-point numbers, strings, and arrays.
- Operators: C# has a range of operators that can be used for arithmetic, comparison, and logical operations.
- Control Flow: C# has control flow statements that allow you to control the flow of execution in a program, including if-else statements, switch statements, loops, and jump statements.
- Functions: Functions are used to group related statements together and reuse code. In C#, you can declare functions using the **public** or **private** access modifier.

Example of Variables and Data Types in C#:

```csharp
using System;

class VariablesAndDataTypes
{
    static void Main(string[] args)
    {
        // Declare an integer variable
        int myInteger = 10;

        // Declare a string variable
        string myString = "Hello, World!";
```

```csharp
        // Declare a boolean variable
        bool myBoolean = true;

        // Print the variables to the console
        Console.WriteLine("Integer: " + myInteger);
        Console.WriteLine("String: " + myString);
        Console.WriteLine("Boolean: " + myBoolean);
    }
}
```

This example demonstrates how to declare variables and data types in C#.

Example of Operators in C#:

```csharp
using System;

class Operators
{
    static void Main(string[] args)
    {
        // Declare two integer variables
        int a = 10;
        int b = 5;

        // Perform arithmetic operations
        int sum = a + b;
        int difference = a - b;
        int product = a * b;
        int quotient = a / b;

        // Print the results to the console
        Console.WriteLine("Sum: " + sum);
        Console.WriteLine("Difference: " + difference);
        Console.WriteLine("Product: " + product);
        Console.WriteLine("Quotient: " + quotient);
    }
}
```

This example demonstrates how to use operators in C#.

Example of Control Flow Statements in C#:

```csharp
using System;

class ControlFlow
{
    static void Main(string[] args)
    {
        // Declare an integer variable
        int myInteger = 10;

        // Use an if-else statement
        if (myInteger > 5)
        {
            Console.WriteLine("myInteger is greater than 5");
        }
        else
        {
            Console.WriteLine("myInteger is less than or equal to 5");
        }

        // Use a switch statement
        switch (myInteger)
        {
            case 10:
                Console.WriteLine("myInteger is 10");
                break;
            case 5:
                Console.WriteLine("myInteger is 5");
                break;
            default:
                Console.WriteLine("myInteger is not 10 or 5");
                break;
        }

        // Use a for loop
```

```csharp
        for (int i = 0; i < 5; i++)
        {
            Console.WriteLine("Iteration: " + i);
        }
    }
}
```

This example demonstrates how to use control flow statements in C#.

Example of Functions in C#:

```csharp
using System;

class Functions
{
    static void Main(string[] args)
    {
        // Declare an integer variable
        int myInteger = 10;

        // Call a function
        int result = Add(myInteger, 5);

        // Print the result to the console
        Console.WriteLine("Result: " + result);
    }

    static int Add(int a, int b)
    {
        return a + b;
    }
}
```

This example demonstrates how to declare and call functions in C#.

2.4 Introduction to Libraries and NuGet Packages

C# is a modern, object-oriented programming language that is designed to work with the .NET Framework. The .NET Framework provides a large set of libraries and APIs for building Windows-based applications, including libraries for file I/O, networking, database access, and user interface development.

In addition to the .NET Framework libraries, C# developers can also use NuGet packages to add functionality to their applications. NuGet packages are pre-built libraries that can be easily installed and used in C# projects. They provide a wide range of functionality, including data access, networking, security, and user interface components.

Example of Using Newtonsoft.Json NuGet Package:

```csharp
using System;
using Newtonsoft.Json;

class JsonExample
{
    static void Main(string[] args)
    {
        // Create a JSON string
        string jsonString = "{\"Name\":\"John Doe\",\"Age\":30}";

        // Deserialize the JSON string into a C# object
        dynamic jsonData = JsonConvert.DeserializeObject(jsonString);

        // Print the C# object to the console
        Console.WriteLine("Name: " + jsonData.Name);
        Console.WriteLine("Age: " + jsonData.Age);
    }
}
```

This example demonstrates how to use the Newtonsoft.Json NuGet package to deserialize a JSON string into a C# object.

Example of Using EntityFramework NuGet Package:

```csharp
using System;
using Microsoft.EntityFrameworkCore;

class EntityFrameworkExample
```

```csharp
{
    static void Main(string[] args)
    {
        // Create a database context
        using (var dbContext = new MyDbContext())
        {
            // Create a new entity
            var entity = new MyEntity { Name = "John Doe", Age = 30 };

            // Add the entity to the database context
            dbContext.MyEntities.Add(entity);

            // Save the changes to the database
            dbContext.SaveChanges();
        }
    }
}

public class MyDbContext : DbContext
{
    public DbSet<MyEntity> MyEntities { get; set; }
}

public class MyEntity
{
    public int Id { get; set; }
    public string Name { get; set; }
    public int Age { get; set; }
}
```

This example demonstrates how to use the EntityFramework NuGet package to create a database context and add an entity to the database.

2.5 Object-Oriented Programming (OOP) in C#

Why OOP is Important

Object-Oriented Programming (OOP) is a fundamental concept in software development that has revolutionized the way we design, develop, and maintain software systems. OOP is important for several reasons:

1. Modularity: OOP allows you to break down a complex system into smaller, independent modules (classes, objects, etc.) that can be easily maintained, updated, and reused. This modularity makes it easier to:

- Develop and test individual components
- Make changes to the system without affecting other parts
- Reuse code in other projects

2. Code Reusability: OOP enables you to write code that can be reused across multiple projects, reducing code duplication and improving development efficiency. By creating reusable classes, objects, and methods, you can:

- Save time and effort by avoiding duplicate code
- Improve code quality and reliability
- Reduce maintenance costs

3. Abstraction: OOP allows you to abstract away complex details and focus on the essential features of a system. Abstraction helps to:

- Simplify complex systems by hiding irrelevant details
- Improve code readability and maintainability
- Reduce the risk of errors and bugs

4. Encapsulation: OOP enables you to encapsulate data and behavior, protecting them from external interference and misuse. Encapsulation helps to:

- Hide internal implementation details from external users
- Prevent data corruption and inconsistencies
- Improve code security and reliability

5. Inheritance: OOP allows you to create a hierarchy of classes, where a subclass inherits the properties and behavior of a parent class. Inheritance helps to:

- Reuse code and behavior from parent classes
- Create a more organized and structured codebase
- Improve code maintainability and scalability

6. Polymorphism: OOP enables you to write code that can work with different types of data and objects, making it more flexible and adaptable. Polymorphism helps to:

- Write more generic and reusable code
- Improve code flexibility and scalability
- Reduce the need for explicit type checking and casting

7. Easier Maintenance and Updates: OOP makes it easier to maintain and update software systems by:

- Providing a clear and organized code structure

- Allowing for modular updates and changes
- Reducing the risk of introducing bugs and errors

8. Improved Collaboration: OOP facilitates collaboration among developers by:

- Providing a common language and framework
- Enabling multiple developers to work on different parts of the system
- Improving communication and coordination among team members

9. Better Error Handling and Debugging: OOP helps to identify and handle errors more effectively by:

- Providing a more structured and organized codebase
- Enabling better error handling and exception management
- Reducing the risk of errors and bugs

10. Improved Scalability and Performance: OOP enables you to write more efficient and scalable code by:

- Providing a more modular and reusable code structure
- Enabling better optimization and performance tuning
- Reducing the risk of performance bottlenecks and scalability issues

In summary, OOP is important because it provides a powerful and flexible framework for designing, developing, and maintaining software systems. By applying OOP principles, developers can create more modular, reusable, and maintainable code, which leads to improved productivity, efficiency, and quality.

1. Classes and Objects:

Create a WebPage class to represent a web page and a WebScraper class to represent the web scraper. The WebPage class will have properties for the page's URL, HTML content, and a method to extract relevant data. The WebScraper class will have a method to scrape the web page.

public class WebPage

{

   public string Url { **get; set;** }

   public string HtmlContent { **get; set;** }

   public WebPage(string url)

```csharp
{
    Url = url;
}

public void LoadHtmlContent()
{
    // Load the HTML content of the web page
    HtmlContent = LoadHtmlFromUrl(Url);
}

private string LoadHtmlFromUrl(string url)
{
    // Use a library like HttpClient to load the HTML content
    using (var client = new HttpClient())
    {
        return client.GetStringAsync(url).Result;
    }
}

public string ExtractTitle()
{
    // Extract the title of the web page
    var titleNode = GetTitleNode(HtmlContent);
    return titleNode.InnerText;
}
```

```csharp
    private HtmlNode GetTitleNode(string htmlContent)
    {
        // Use a library like HtmlAgilityPack to parse the HTML content
        var doc = new HtmlDocument();
        doc.LoadHtml(htmlContent);
        return doc.DocumentNode.SelectSingleNode("//title");
    }
}

public class WebScraper
{
    public WebPage WebPage { get; set; }

    public WebScraper(string url)
    {
        WebPage = new WebPage(url);
    }

    public void ScrapeWebPage()
    {
        WebPage.LoadHtmlContent();
        var title = WebPage.ExtractTitle();
        Console.WriteLine($"Title: {title}");
    }
```

}

2. Inheritance:

Create a NewsWebScraper class that inherits from the WebScraper class.
The NewsWebScraper class will have additional methods to extract news articles from the web page.

public class NewsWebScraper : WebScraper

{

  public NewsWebScraper(string url) : **base**(url)

  {

  }

  public void ExtractNewsArticles()

  {

    var articles = WebPage.ExtractNewsArticles();

    foreach (**var** article **in** articles)

    {

      Console.WriteLine($"Article: {article}");

    }

  }

}

public class WebPage

{

  //... existing code...

  public string[] **ExtractNewsArticles**()

```csharp
    {
        // Extract news articles from the web page
        var articleNodes = GetArticleNodes(HtmlContent);
        var articles = new string[articleNodes.Count];
        for (int i = 0; i < articleNodes.Count; i++)
        {
            articles[i] = articleNodes[i].InnerText;
        }
        return articles;
    }

    private HtmlNodeCollection GetArticleNodes(string htmlContent)
    {
        // Use a library like HtmlAgilityPack to parse the HTML content
        var doc = new HtmlDocument();
        doc.LoadHtml(htmlContent);
        return doc.DocumentNode.SelectNodes("//article");
    }
}
```

3. Polymorphism:

Create an IWebScraper interface that defines the ScrapeWebPage method.
The WebScraper class will implement this interface. Create a NewsWebScraper class that also implements this interface. This allows you to use polymorphism to scrape different types of web pages.

```csharp
public interface IWebScraper
{
```

```csharp
    void ScrapeWebPage();
}


public class WebScraper : IWebScraper
{
    //... existing code...

    public void ScrapeWebPage()
    {
        WebPage.LoadHtmlContent();
        var title = WebPage.ExtractTitle();
        Console.WriteLine($"Title: {title}");
    }
}


public class NewsWebScraper : WebScraper, IWebScraper
{
    //... existing code...

    public void ScrapeWebPage()
    {
        base.ScrapeWebPage();
        ExtractNewsArticles();
    }
}
```

4. Encapsulation:

Encapsulate the data and behavior of the WebPage class by making its properties and methods private or protected. This helps to hide the implementation details of the class from the outside world.

```csharp
public class WebPage
{
    private string url;

    private string htmlContent;

    public WebPage(string url)
    {
        this.url = url;
    }

    protected void LoadHtmlContent()
    {
        // Load the HTML content of the web page
        htmlContent = LoadHtmlFromUrl(url);
    }

    private string LoadHtmlFromUrl(string url)
    {
        // Use a library like HttpClient to load the HTML content
        using (var client = new HttpClient())
        {
            return client.GetStringAsync(url).Result;
```

```csharp
        }
    }


    public string ExtractTitle()
    {
        // Extract the title of the web page
        var titleNode = GetTitleNode(htmlContent);
        return titleNode.InnerText;
    }


    private HtmlNode GetTitleNode(string htmlContent)
    {
        // Use a library like HtmlAgilityPack to parse the HTML content
        var doc = new HtmlDocument();
        doc.LoadHtml(htmlContent);
        return doc.DocumentNode.SelectSingleNode("//title");
    }
}
```

5. Abstraction:

Abstract the WebScraper class by creating an IWebScraper interface that defines the ScrapeWebPage method. This allows you to use different types of web scrapers without knowing the implementation details.

```csharp
public interface IWebScraper
{
    void ScrapeWebPage();
}
```

public class WebScraper : IWebScraper

{

   //... existing code...

}

In conclusion, Object-Oriented Programming (OOP) is a fundamental concept in C# that helps you write reusable, modular, and maintainable code. By applying OOP principles such as classes and objects, inheritance, polymorphism, encapsulation, and abstraction, you can create robust and scalable web scrapers. Web scraping is the process of automatically extracting data from websites, and it has numerous applications in data mining, market research, and more. By using OOP principles, you can create web scrapers that can handle different types of websites, extract relevant data, and store it in a structured format. Additionally, OOP principles help to reduce code duplication, improve code readability, and increase code flexibility, making it easier to maintain and update your web scraper codebase.

Some of the benefits of using OOP principles in web scraping include:

- **Modularity**: OOP principles allow you to break down your web scraper code into smaller, independent modules that can be easily maintained and updated.
- **Reusability**: OOP principles enable you to reuse code across different web scrapers, reducing code duplication and improving code efficiency.
- **Flexibility**: OOP principles allow you to create web scrapers that can handle different types of websites and extract relevant data, making it easier to adapt to changing website structures and data formats.
- **Scalability**: OOP principles enable you to create web scrapers that can handle large volumes of data and scale to meet the needs of your application.

Some popular libraries and frameworks for web scraping in C# include:

- **HtmlAgilityPack**: A library for parsing HTML and XML documents.
- **HttpClient**: A library for sending HTTP requests and receiving HTTP responses.
- **Scrapy**: A framework for building web scrapers that provides a flexible and efficient way to extract data from websites.

Overall, OOP principles are essential for building robust and scalable web scrapers in C#. By applying these principles, you can create web scrapers that can handle different types of websites, extract relevant data, and store it in a structured format, making it easier to maintain and update your web scraper codebase.

In conclusion, C# is a powerful and versatile language that is well-suited for building a wide range of software systems. Its syntax and concepts are based on the C and C++ programming languages, but it has many additional features and improvements that make it a more efficient and effective language for building Windows-based applications. With the.NET Framework and NuGet packages, C# developers have access to a wide range of libraries and APIs that can be used to add functionality to their applications. Whether you're building a Windows desktop application, a web application, or a mobile app, C# is a great choice for any development project.

Chapter 3: HTTP , the Protocol of Internet

3.1Understanding HTTP and HTML
How the Web Works: HTTP and HTTPS Protocols

The Hypertext Transfer Protocol (HTTP) is the foundation of data communication on the World Wide Web. HTTP is a protocol used for transmitting data between a client (usually a web browser) and a server. It is a request-response protocol that facilitates the transfer of documents, images, videos, and other resources over the web.

HTTP Request and Response

- **Request**: A client, such as a web browser, sends an HTTP request to the server when a user tries to access a website or resource. The request consists of:
  - **Request line**: Includes the method (GET, POST, PUT, DELETE, etc.), the URL, and the HTTP version.
  - **Headers**: Provide additional information like the type of content being requested, the user agent, and any cookies.
  - **Body**: Some requests (e.g., POST) include a body that contains data, such as form submissions.
- **Response**: The server responds to the client's request with an HTTP response, which includes:
  - **Status code**: Indicates the result of the request (e.g., 200 OK, 404 Not Found, 500 Internal Server Error).
  - **Headers**: Provide information such as the content type (HTML, JSON, etc.) and caching policies.
  - **Body**: Contains the requested resource, typically in the form of HTML, JSON, or images.

The HTTP Request-Response Lifecycle

1. A user enters a URL in the browser, initiating an HTTP request.
2. The request is routed via DNS (Domain Name System) to the server hosting the requested resource.
3. The server processes the request and sends back an HTTP response.
4. The client (browser) processes the response and renders the content (e.g., displays the HTML page).

HTTPS (Hypertext Transfer Protocol Secure): HTTPS is the secure version of HTTP. It encrypts the data transmitted between the client and the server using SSL/TLS (Secure Socket Layer/Transport Layer Security). This ensures that sensitive information, such as login credentials and payment details, cannot be intercepted during transmission. HTTPS is essential for protecting privacy and integrity of data over the internet.

SSL/TLS Encryption: HTTPS uses encryption to protect the data from third parties. SSL/TLS protocols secure the data by encrypting it at both ends (client and server).

Trust and Authentication: HTTPS also involves the use of certificates issued by trusted Certificate Authorities (CAs) to ensure that the server being connected to is legitimate. When a user visits an HTTPS website, the browser checks the server's SSL certificate to confirm its authenticity.

Why HTTPS is Important

- **Data Security**: HTTPS encrypts data to prevent eavesdropping and tampering.
- **SEO Ranking**: Search engines like Google give preference to HTTPS websites in their search results, improving visibility.

- **User Trust**: Websites with HTTPS are more trustworthy, as browsers display a padlock icon in the address bar.

In summary, the HTTP and HTTPS protocols form the backbone of web communication, ensuring that data is sent and received between the client and the server, and HTTPS adds an important layer of security.

3.2 HTML: The Language of Web Pages

HTML (Hypertext Markup Language) is the standard language used to create and structure content on the web. HTML is not a programming language but a markup language that defines the structure of web pages. HTML uses a system of tags to define elements such as headings, paragraphs, links, images, tables, and more.

Basic Structure of HTML: An HTML document starts with a <!DOCTYPE html> declaration, followed by the root element <html>. Within the <html> tag, the document is divided into two main parts:

- **Head** (<head>): Contains metadata about the document such as the title, character encoding, links to external resources (CSS, JavaScript), and other information.

```
<head>
 <meta charset="UTF-8">
 <title>My Web Page</title>
</head>
```

- **Body** (<body>): Contains the content of the page that is displayed to users, such as text, images, forms, etc.

```
<body>
 <h1>Welcome to My Web Page</h1>
 <p>This is a paragraph of text.</p>
</body>
```

Common HTML Tags

- <h1> to <h6>: Header tags define headings with <h1> being the highest level and <h6> the lowest.
- <p>: Paragraph tag is used to define blocks of text.
- <a>: Anchor tag is used to define hyperlinks.

```
<a href="https://www.example.com">Click Here</a>
```

- `<img>`: Image tag is used to embed images on the page.

`<img src="image.jpg" alt="An example image">`

- `<ul>`, `<ol>`, `<li>`: Tags for unordered and ordered lists.

```
<ul>
 <li>Item 1</li>
 <li>Item 2</li>
</ul>
```

- `<div>` and `<span>`: Div and span are container elements used for grouping other elements. `<div>` is a block-level element, while `<span>` is inline.

```
<div>
 <h2>Header</h2>
 <p>Paragraph inside a div.</p>
</div>
```

Forms in HTML: Forms allow users to submit data to a server. HTML provides form elements like text fields, checkboxes, radio buttons, and submit buttons.

```
<form action="/submit" method="POST">
 <label for="name">Name:</label>
 <input type="text" id="name" name="name">
 <input type="submit" value="Submit">
</form>
```

HTML5 Features: HTML5 introduced new semantic elements that improve accessibility and search engine optimization:

- `<header>`: Defines the header section of a page.
- `<article>`: Defines an independent section of content.
- `<section>`: Defines sections of content that can be independently grouped.
- `<footer>`: Defines the footer section of a page.
- `<aside>`: Defines content that is tangentially related to the content around it.

In conclusion, HTML is a markup language that structures the content of web pages, making it possible for browsers to render and display the content correctly.

Basics of DOM (Document Object Model)

The Document Object Model (DOM) is a programming interface for web documents. It represents the page so that programs can manipulate its structure, style, and content dynamically. The DOM treats the web page as a tree structure where each element (HTML tag) is a node.

DOM Structure

- **Document**: The root of the DOM tree, representing the entire document.
- **Elements**: Each HTML tag is represented as an element node.
- **Text Nodes**: Each piece of text inside an element is represented as a text node.
- **Attributes**: HTML attributes (like id, class, href) are also represented as nodes attached to elements.

Example DOM Representation: For an HTML document:

```html
<!DOCTYPE html>
<html>
 <head>
  <title>Document</title>
 </head>
 <body>
  <h1>My Web Page</h1>
  <p>Welcome to my website.</p>
 </body>
</html>
```

The corresponding DOM structure:

```
Document
 ├── html
 │   ├── head
 │   │   └── title (Document)
 │   └── body
 │       ├── h1 (My Web Page)
 │       └── p (Welcome to my website.)
```

Accessing DOM Elements: JavaScript provides several methods to access and manipulate elements in the DOM:

- getElementById(): Access an element by its ID.

```
const element = document.getElementById('myId');
```

- getElementsByTagName(): Access all elements with a specific tag name.

```
const paragraphs = document.getElementsByTagName('p');
```

- querySelector(): Access the first element matching a CSS selector.

```
const header = document.querySelector('h1');
```

Manipulating DOM Elements: You can change the content or style of elements in the DOM using JavaScript:

- **Changing Text Content**: You can change the text inside an element using .textContent or .innerText.

```
document.getElementById('myId').textContent = 'New text content';
```

- **Changing Styles**: You can modify the CSS properties of an element using .style.

```
document.getElementById('myId').style.color = 'red';
```

DOM Events: DOM events allow interaction with users. Some common events include:

- **Click**: Triggered when an element is clicked.
- **Load**: Triggered when the page finishes loading.
- **Submit**: Triggered when a form is submitted.

Example of Handling a DOM Event:

```
document.getElementById('myButton').addEventListener('click', function() {
  alert('Button clicked!');
});
```

In conclusion, the DOM is a critical part of web development, enabling developers to interact with the content, structure, and styles of web pages dynamically.

3.3 Tools for Inspecting and Analyzing Web Pages

To effectively work with web pages, developers need tools to inspect and analyze their structure, performance, and behavior. Several powerful tools are available, often built directly into web browsers.

1. Browser Developer Tools (DevTools): Most modern browsers, including Google Chrome, Mozilla Firefox, and Microsoft Edge, come with built-in Developer Tools. These tools allow developers to inspect HTML and CSS, debug JavaScript, monitor network requests, and analyze page performance.

Key Features of DevTools

- **Elements Panel**: Allows you to view and modify the HTML and CSS of a page. You can live-edit styles, view element attributes, and even test changes in real-time.
- **Console Panel**: Displays messages, errors, and logs generated by JavaScript. You can also execute JavaScript directly from this panel.
- **Network Panel**: Shows all network requests made by the page, including HTML, CSS, JavaScript, images, and API calls. It helps in debugging performance issues like slow loading times.
- **Performance Panel**: Analyzes the performance of your page by recording and visualizing its runtime. It shows things like page load time, JavaScript execution time, and rendering time.
- **Sources Panel**: Allows you to view and debug JavaScript files. It includes features like setting breakpoints and stepping through the code to identify issues.

2. Lighthouse: Google Lighthouse is an open-source tool for auditing web page performance, accessibility, SEO, and best practices. It provides a detailed report and suggestions on how to improve the site.
3. WebPageTest: WebPageTest is an online tool that tests the performance of web pages from different locations and devices. It provides detailed insights into page load times, rendering performance, and network requests.
4. Fiddler: Fiddler is a free web debugging proxy tool used to capture and inspect HTTP(S) traffic. It is helpful for analyzing how web pages interact with servers and identifying any issues with network requests.
5. Chrome Extensions: There are various browser extensions available for inspecting and analyzing web pages, including:

- Wappalyzer: Identifies technologies used by a website (e.g., CMS, JavaScript frameworks, analytics tools).
- BuiltWith: Analyzes the technology stack of websites, including server details and analytics tools.

In conclusion, these tools help developers inspect, debug, and analyze various aspects of a web page, from structure to performance. Mastery of these tools is essential for optimizing user experience, improving web performance, and troubleshooting issues efficiently.

Chapter 4: Core Libraries for Web Scraping in C#

4.1 Overview of HttpClient for HTTP Requests

Web scraping begins with sending an HTTP request to a website and retrieving the HTML content of the page. The HttpClient class in C# is a powerful tool to manage these HTTP requests. It allows asynchronous communication, meaning you can perform multiple requests without blocking your main application thread. Let's break down the key aspects of HttpClient and its usage:

Key Features of HttpClient

1. **Asynchronous Programming**: HttpClient uses asynchronous methods like GetAsync(), PostAsync(), which are non-blocking. This allows your program to send multiple requests at once without waiting for each one to complete sequentially.
2. **Multiple HTTP Methods**: HttpClient supports various HTTP request types such as GET, POST, PUT, DELETE, and others. This is useful for interacting with REST APIs, submitting forms, or making API requests.
3. **Request Headers**: HTTP headers are essential to mimic real user requests (for example, setting the User-Agent to make requests look like they come from a browser). HttpClient lets you customize headers easily.
4. **Response Handling**: HttpClient handles responses in multiple formats like JSON, XML, or HTML. It also provides robust error handling and status code checking.

Code Example using HttpClient

```csharp
using System;
using System.Net.Http;
using System.Threading.Tasks;

public class Program
{
    public static async Task Main()
    {
        var client = new HttpClient();

        try
        {
            // Send a GET request to the webpage
            var response = await client.GetAsync("https://www.example.com");

            // Check if the request was successful
            if (response.IsSuccessStatusCode)
            {
                // Read the HTML content of the response
                var html = await response.Content.ReadAsStringAsync();

                // Output the HTML content
                Console.WriteLine(html);
            }
            else
            {
                Console.WriteLine($"Error: {response.StatusCode}");
            }
        }
        catch (Exception ex)
        {
            Console.WriteLine($"Exception: {ex.Message}");
        }
        finally
        {
            // Ensure the HttpClient instance is disposed properly
            client.Dispose();
        }
    }
}
```

This code sends an asynchronous GET request to the specified URL and checks if the request is successful (status code 200). If successful, it outputs the HTML content.

4.2 Using HtmlAgilityPack for Parsing HTML

Once you've fetched the HTML of a webpage using HttpClient, the next step is to parse that HTML and extract meaningful data. This is where HtmlAgilityPack comes into play. It is a lightweight, easy-to-use library that parses HTML and allows easy manipulation of HTML nodes.

Key Features of HtmlAgilityPack

1. **HTML Parsing**: The library loads the HTML content into a HtmlDocument object, which provides a hierarchical representation of the HTML structure. This allows you to easily traverse and manipulate HTML nodes.
2. **XPath and LINQ Support**: You can use XPath queries to select elements, or you can use LINQ to filter and extract content in a more C#-centric way.
3. **Node Selection**: HtmlAgilityPack supports searching for nodes by tag name, attribute, or class, making it easy to extract specific pieces of data.
4. **Attribute Extraction**: You can extract attributes like href, src, and alt from elements such as links (<a>) or images (<img>).

Code Example using HtmlAgilityPack

```
using System;
using HtmlAgilityPack;
using System.Net.Http;
using System.Threading.Tasks;

public class Program
{
    public static async Task Main()
    {
        var client = new HttpClient();

        try
        {
            // Send a GET request to the webpage
            var response = await client.GetAsync("https://www.example.com");

            // Check if the request was successful
            if (response.IsSuccessStatusCode)
            {
                // Read the HTML content
                var html = await response.Content.ReadAsStringAsync();

                // Create a new HtmlDocument to parse the HTML content
                var doc = new HtmlDocument();
                doc.LoadHtml(html);

                // Select all paragraph nodes <p>
                var paragraphs = doc.DocumentNode.SelectNodes("//p");

                if (paragraphs != null)
                {
                    foreach (var paragraph in paragraphs)
                    {
                        Console.WriteLine(paragraph.InnerText);
                    }
                }
                else
                {
                    Console.WriteLine("No paragraphs found.");
```

```
                }
            }
            else
            {
                Console.WriteLine($"Error: {response.StatusCode}");
            }
        }
        catch (Exception ex)
        {
            Console.WriteLine($"Exception: {ex.Message}");
        }
        finally
        {
            client.Dispose();
        }
    }
}
```

This code demonstrates how to parse the HTML content and extract text from `<p>` tags. The `SelectNodes` method uses XPath to find all paragraph nodes and outputs their inner text.

4.3 Exploring AngleSharp for Advanced Scraping

`AngleSharp` is another advanced library for parsing HTML and CSS in C#. It is more modern and efficient than `HtmlAgilityPack`, offering better performance, especially with complex documents.

Key Features of AngleSharp

1. **HTML and CSS Parsing**: AngleSharp parses both HTML and CSS, allowing you to access and manipulate elements based on their styles, such as extracting hidden elements or determining if a specific style rule applies.
2. **QuerySelector API**: Similar to JavaScript's `querySelector` method, `AngleSharp` allows you to select elements using CSS selectors, which is more intuitive and similar to browser-based JavaScript.
3. **DOM Manipulation**: AngleSharp allows for real-time manipulation of the DOM, such as adding, removing, or changing nodes. This is more advanced compared to `HtmlAgilityPack`, which only supports static DOM manipulation.
4. **Browser-Like Functionality**: AngleSharp provides a more accurate parsing of HTML and CSS, mimicking a real browser's behavior. This includes handling character encoding, link resolution, and CSS computation.

Code Example using AngleSharp

```
using System;
using AngleSharp;
using System.Net.Http;
using System.Threading.Tasks;

public class Program
```

```
{
    public static async Task Main()
    {
        var client = new HttpClient();

        try
        {
            // Send a GET request to the webpage
            var response = await client.GetAsync("https://www.example.com");

            // Check if the request was successful
            if (response.IsSuccessStatusCode)
            {
                // Read the HTML content
                var html = await response.Content.ReadAsStringAsync();

                // Initialize AngleSharp configuration and context
                var config = Configuration.Default;
                var context = BrowsingContext.New(config);

                // Parse the HTML content
                var document = await context.OpenAsync(req => req.Content(html));

                // Select all paragraphs <p> using CSS selector
                var paragraphs = document.QuerySelectorAll("p");

                foreach (var paragraph in paragraphs)
                {
                    Console.WriteLine(paragraph.TextContent);
                }
            }
            else
            {
                Console.WriteLine($"Error: {response.StatusCode}");
            }
        }
        catch (Exception ex)
        {
            Console.WriteLine($"Exception: {ex.Message}");
        }
        finally
        {
            client.Dispose();
        }
    }
}
```

This code uses AngleSharp to fetch and parse HTML, and it outputs the content of all paragraph tags (<p>) using the QuerySelectorAll method.

4.5 Handling Dynamic Content

Many modern websites use JavaScript to load data dynamically, which traditional HTTP requests may not capture. To handle dynamic content, tools like **Selenium** or **Playwright** can be integrated with C#. These tools allow you to control a web browser (e.g., Chrome) programmatically, enabling you to scrape data even if it requires interacting with JavaScript.

Selenium Example (Basic)

```csharp
using OpenQA.Selenium;
using OpenQA.Selenium.Chrome;
using System;

class Program
{
    static void Main()
    {
        var driver = new ChromeDriver();
        driver.Navigate().GoToUrl("https://www.example.com");

        // Wait for the page to load (or use more advanced waits)
        var element = driver.FindElement(By.TagName("p"));
        Console.WriteLine(element.Text);

        driver.Quit();
    }
}
```

4.6 Best Practices for Web Scraping

1. **Respect Robots.txt**: Always check the robots.txt file of a website to ensure you're not violating any scraping rules.
2. **Rate Limiting**: To avoid overwhelming a server, add rate limiting (delays between requests) or implement an exponential backoff strategy.
3. **Error Handling**: Proper error handling for network issues, server errors, or changes in the HTML structure is essential for creating a resilient scraper.
4. **Legal Considerations**: Ensure that your web scraping activities comply with the legal terms of the website you're scraping. Always review the website's terms of service.

Conclusion

In summary, HttpClient, HtmlAgilityPack, and AngleSharp are all excellent tools for building a web scraper in C#. Each has its own strengths depending on your needs. Combining these libraries allows you to fetch HTML, parse it, and extract meaningful data effectively. Additionally, using tools like Selenium or Playwright can help in handling dynamic content, ensuring your scraper works even on modern, JavaScript-heavy websites.

Chapter 5: Building Your First Web Scraper

Before we dive into the exciting world of web scraping, I want to ensure that you, the reader, are prepared for the journey ahead. In the previous chapters, we explored the treasure trove of data available on the internet, learned the basics of C#, and gained a deep understanding of HTTP, HTML, and the tools used for inspecting and analyzing web pages. We also introduced you to the core libraries used for web scraping in C#, including HttpClient, HtmlAgilityPack, and AngleSharp.

As we move forward, it's essential to have a solid grasp of the concepts covered in the previous chapters. If you're new to web scraping or C#, I recommend taking a moment to review the earlier sections to ensure you're comfortable with the material. Don't worry if you need to take a step back – it's better to build a strong foundation now than to struggle later on.

With that said, let's embark on the next phase of our journey: building your first web scraper! In this chapter, we'll take a hands-on approach, guiding you through the process of setting up your project, fetching web pages, and extracting data using HtmlAgilityPack.

Setting Up Your Project: A Step-by-Step Guide

To start, you'll need to create a new project in Visual Studio. If you're not familiar with Visual Studio, don't worry – we'll walk through the process together. To create a new project, follow these steps:

1. Open Visual Studio, and click on "Create a new project" on the start page.
2. In the search bar, type "Console App (.NET Core)" and select the result.
3. Choose a name for your project, such as "WebScraperExample."
4. Select a location to save your project, and click "Create."
5. In the Solution Explorer, right-click on the project and select "Manage NuGet Packages."
6. Search for "HtmlAgilityPack" and install the package.
7. Repeat the process for "System.Net.Http" to install the HttpClient package.

With your project set up, you're ready to start building your web scraper. Take a moment to familiarize yourself with theSolution Explorer, which displays the structure of your project.

5.1 Fetching Web Pages with HttpClient

Now that your project is set up, it's time to fetch your first web page using HttpClient. HttpClient is a powerful class that allows you to send HTTP requests to web servers and retrieve the responses. To use HttpClient, you'll need to create an instance of the class and specify the URL of the web page you want to fetch.

Here's an example of how to use HttpClient to fetch a web page:
Fetching and Parsing Inline Links

```
using System;

using System.Net.Http;

using System.Threading.Tasks;

using HtmlAgilityPack;


class Program

{

  static async Task Main(string[] args)

  {
```

```csharp
        string url = "https://example.com";
        await CrawlPage(url);
    }

    static async Task CrawlPage(string baseUrl)
    {
        HttpClient httpClient = new HttpClient();
        try
        {
            // Fetch the main page
            var response = await httpClient.GetAsync(baseUrl);
            if (response.IsSuccessStatusCode)
            {
                var htmlContent = await response.Content.ReadAsStringAsync();

                // Load HTML content
                HtmlDocument htmlDoc = new HtmlDocument();
                htmlDoc.LoadHtml(htmlContent);

                // Find all <a> elements with href attributes
                var linkNodes = htmlDoc.DocumentNode.SelectNodes("//a[@href]");
                if (linkNodes != null)
                {
                    Console.WriteLine("Extracted Links:");
                    foreach (var link in linkNodes)
                    {
                        string linkHref = link.GetAttributeValue("href", string.Empty);
                        Console.WriteLine(linkHref);
                    }
                }
                else
```

```csharp
            {
                Console.WriteLine("No links found on the page.");
            }


            // Check for robots.txt and sitemap.xml
            await CheckForRobotsAndSitemap(baseUrl);
        }
    }
    catch (Exception ex)
    {
        Console.WriteLine($"An error occurred: {ex.Message}");
    }
}


static async Task CheckForRobotsAndSitemap(string baseUrl)
{
    HttpClient httpClient = new HttpClient();

    // Check for robots.txt
    string robotsUrl = $"{baseUrl.TrimEnd('/')}/robots.txt";
    Console.WriteLine($"\nChecking for robots.txt at: {robotsUrl}");
    var robotsResponse = await httpClient.GetAsync(robotsUrl);
    if (robotsResponse.IsSuccessStatusCode)
    {
        var robotsContent = await robotsResponse.Content.ReadAsStringAsync();
        Console.WriteLine("robots.txt content:");
        Console.WriteLine(robotsContent);
    }
    else
    {
        Console.WriteLine("robots.txt not found.");
```

```csharp
    }

    // Check for sitemap.xml
    string sitemapUrl = $"{baseUrl.TrimEnd('/')}/sitemap.xml";
    Console.WriteLine($"\nChecking for sitemap.xml at: {sitemapUrl}");
    var sitemapResponse = await httpClient.GetAsync(sitemapUrl);
    if (sitemapResponse.IsSuccessStatusCode)
    {
        Console.WriteLine("Sitemap found:");
        Console.WriteLine(sitemapUrl);
    }
    else
    {
        Console.WriteLine("Sitemap not found.");
    }
  }
}
```

Code Explanation

1. **Crawl Inline Links**:
    - The SelectNodes("//a[@href]") XPath expression selects all <a> tags with an href attribute.
    - GetAttributeValue("href", string.Empty) retrieves the URL value of the href attribute.
2. **Robots.txt**:
    - The scraper constructs the URL by appending /robots.txt to the base URL.
    - If found, it displays the content, helping ensure the scraper respects the site's rules.
3. **Sitemap.xml**:
    - Similarly, it looks for /sitemap.xml, a standard way to discover structured URLs for the website.

Advanced XPath Syntax Examples

- **XPath to Select Specific Attributes**:

- o   //a[@href]: Selects all <a> elements with an href attribute.
- o   //img[@src]: Selects all <img> elements with a src attribute.

- **Filtering Nodes**:
    - o   //a[contains(@href, 'example')]: Selects <a> elements whose href attribute contains the word "example".
    - o   //div[@class='content']: Selects <div> elements with a class attribute equal to "content".

- **Combining XPath**:
    - o   //a | //img: Selects all <a> and <img> elements.

- **Parent-Child Relationships**:
    - o   //div/p: Selects all <p> elements inside <div> elements.

Exercises to Try

1. Modify the crawler to filter out external links by checking whether href starts with the base URL.
2. Extend the CrawlPage method to follow each extracted link and scrape data recursively, respecting robots.txt rules.

5.2 Crawling Links from Sitemap and Saving Results
In this section, we will extend the functionality of our scraper to find and parse a sitemap, extract links from it, and save the results into a CSV file for further use.

Code Implementation

```
using System;

using System.Collections.Generic;

using System.IO;

using System.Net.Http;

using System.Threading.Tasks;

using HtmlAgilityPack;


class Program
```

```csharp
{
    static async Task Main(string[] args)
    {
        string baseUrl = "https://example.com";
        await CrawlSitemap(baseUrl);
    }

    static async Task CrawlSitemap(string baseUrl)
    {
        HttpClient httpClient = new HttpClient();
        string sitemapUrl = $"{baseUrl.TrimEnd('/')}/sitemap.xml";

        try
        {
            Console.WriteLine($"Checking for sitemap.xml at: {sitemapUrl}");
            var response = await httpClient.GetAsync(sitemapUrl);

            if (response.IsSuccessStatusCode)
            {
                var sitemapContent = await response.Content.ReadAsStringAsync();

                Console.WriteLine("Sitemap found. Parsing links...");
                var links = ParseSitemap(sitemapContent);

                Console.WriteLine($"Found {links.Count} links in sitemap. Crawling and saving to CSV...");
                await SaveLinksToCsv(links);
            }
            else
            {
                Console.WriteLine("Sitemap not found or inaccessible.");
            }
```

```csharp
            }
            catch (Exception ex)
            {
                Console.WriteLine($"An error occurred while processing the sitemap: {ex.Message}");
            }
        }

        static List<string> ParseSitemap(string sitemapContent)
        {
            List<string> links = new List<string>();
            HtmlDocument htmlDoc = new HtmlDocument();
            htmlDoc.LoadHtml(sitemapContent);

            // Select all <loc> tags inside the sitemap
            var locNodes = htmlDoc.DocumentNode.SelectNodes("//url/loc");

            if (locNodes != null)
            {
                foreach (var node in locNodes)
                {
                    links.Add(node.InnerText.Trim());
                }
            }
            else
            {
                Console.WriteLine("No links found in the sitemap.");
            }

            return links;
        }
```

```csharp
static async Task SaveLinksToCsv(List<string> links)
{
    string filePath = "sitemap_links.csv";

    try
    {
        using (StreamWriter writer = new StreamWriter(filePath))
        {
            // Write CSV header
            await writer.WriteLineAsync("URL");

            // Write each link to the CSV
            foreach (var link in links)
            {
                await writer.WriteLineAsync(link);
            }
        }

        Console.WriteLine($"Links successfully saved to {filePath}");
    }
    catch (Exception ex)
    {
        Console.WriteLine($"An error occurred while saving the CSV: {ex.Message}");
    }
}
```

Code Explanation

1. **Fetching Sitemap:**
    - The CrawlSitemap method constructs the sitemap URL (sitemap.xml) and checks its availability using HttpClient.GetAsync.

2. **Parsing Sitemap:**
   - The ParseSitemap method uses HtmlAgilityPack to parse the sitemap XML.
   - The XPath expression //url/loc selects all <loc> tags, which typically contain URLs in the sitemap.

3. **Saving Links to CSV:**
   - The SaveLinksToCsv method creates a CSV file named sitemap_links.csv.
   - Each extracted link is written as a new row under the "URL" column.

Example of Sitemap Structure

A typical sitemap XML file might look like this:

xml

```xml
<?xml version="1.0" encoding="UTF-8"?>
<urlset xmlns="http://www.sitemaps.org/schemas/sitemap/0.9">
 <url>
  <loc>https://example.com/page1</loc>
 </url>
 <url>
  <loc>https://example.com/page2</loc>
 </url>
</urlset>
```

- The XPath //url/loc identifies each <loc> element within <url> tags.

Enhancements to Consider

- **Recursive Crawling:** After saving the links, extend the program to recursively crawl each URL and extract further data.
- **CSV Enhancements:** Add columns for additional metadata like HTTP status codes or timestamps.
- **Error Handling:** Include better error handling for malformed sitemap files or unexpected formats.

Final Output

When executed:

1. The scraper fetches the sitemap from the provided URL.
2. Extracts all <loc> links.
3. Saves these links into sitemap_links.csv, with one link per line.

CSV Sample:

arduino

URL

https://example.com/page1

https://example.com/page2

In this example, we create a new instance of HttpClient and specify the URL of the web page to fetch. We then send a GET request to the web server using the GetAsync method, which returns a HttpResponseMessage object. We check the status code of the response to ensure it was successful, and if so, we read the content of the response as a string using the ReadAsStringAsync method.

5.3 Extracting Data with HtmlAgilityPack

Now that you've fetched a web page using HttpClient, it's time to extract the data you need using HtmlAgilityPack. HtmlAgilityPack is a powerful library that allows you to parse HTML documents and extract data from them. One of the most powerful features of HtmlAgilityPack is its support for XPath expressions, which allow you to select specific elements within an HTML document.

Introduction to XPath

XPath (XML Path Language) is a language used to navigate and select elements within an XML or HTML document. XPath expressions are used to specify a path to a specific element or set of elements within a document. With HtmlAgilityPack, you can use XPath expressions to select elements within an HTML document and extract the data you need.

Basic XPath Syntax

XPath expressions consist of a series of steps, each separated by a forward slash (/). Each step specifies a node or axis within the document, and can include filters or predicates to narrow down the selection. Here are some basic XPath syntax elements:

- /: root node
- //: descendant node (anywhere in the document)
- ./: current node
- ../: parent node
- @: attribute node
- *: wildcard (matches any element or attribute)

For example, the XPath expression /html/body/h1 would select the h1 element within the body element within the html element.

XPath Axes

XPath axes are used to specify the direction of the selection. The following axes are available:

- ancestor: selects the ancestors of the current node
- ancestor-or-self: selects the current node and its ancestors
- attribute: selects the attributes of the current node
- child: selects the children of the current node
- descendant: selects the descendants of the current node
- descendant-or-self: selects the current node and its descendants
- following: selects the nodes that follow the current node
- following-sibling: selects the siblings of the current node that follow it
- parent: selects the parent of the current node
- preceding: selects the nodes that precede the current node
- preceding-sibling: selects the siblings of the current node that precede it
- self: selects the current node

XPath Functions

XPath functions are used to perform operations on the selected nodes. The following functions are available:

- contains(): tests whether a string contains another string
- count(): returns the number of nodes in the selected set
- id(): returns the node with the specified ID
- last(): returns the last node in the selected set
- name(): returns the name of the selected node
- position(): returns the position of the selected node
- starts-with(): tests whether a string starts with another string
- string(): returns the string value of the selected node

Using XPath with HtmlAgilityPack

To use XPath with HtmlAgilityPack, you can use the SelectNodes method, which takes an XPath expression as a parameter. For example:

```
var htmlDoc = new HtmlDocument();

htmlDoc.LoadHtml(html);


var nodes = htmlDoc.DocumentNode.SelectNodes("//h2");

foreach (var node in nodes)
```

```
{
    Console.WriteLine(node.InnerText);
}
```

In this example, the XPath expression //h2 is used to select all h2 elements within the HTML document. The SelectNodes method returns a collection of nodes that match the XPath expression, which can then be iterated over and processed.

Common XPath Expressions

Here are some common XPath expressions that you may find useful when working with HtmlAgilityPack:

- //a: selects all a elements (links) within the document
- //img: selects all img elements (images) within the document
- //h1: selects all h1 elements (headings) within the document
- //p: selects all p elements (paragraphs) within the document
- //table: selects all table elements within the document
- //tr: selects all tr elements (table rows) within the document
- //td: selects all td elements (table cells) within the document

Combining XPath Expressions

You can combine multiple XPath expressions using the | character, which is used to specify a union of two or more expressions. For example:

var nodes = htmlDoc.DocumentNode.SelectNodes("//h1 | //h2");

In this example, the XPath expression //h1 | //h2 selects all h1 and h2 elements within the document.

By using XPath expressions with HtmlAgilityPack, you can easily select and extract data from HTML documents, even if the structure of the document is complex or unpredictable. With practice and experience, you can become proficient in using XPath to extract data from a wide range of HTML documents.

Example Use Cases

Here are some example use cases for using XPath with HtmlAgilityPack:

- Extracting data from a table: var rows = htmlDoc.DocumentNode.SelectNodes("//table[@id='myTable']/tr");
- Extracting links from a page: var links = htmlDoc.DocumentNode.SelectNodes("//a[@href]");
- Extracting headings from a page: var headings = htmlDoc.DocumentNode.SelectNodes("//h1 | //h2 | //h3");
- Extracting images from a page: var images = htmlDoc.DocumentNode.SelectNodes("//img[@src]");

These are just a few examples of the many use cases for using XPath with HtmlAgilityPack. By mastering XPath, you can unlock the full potential of HtmlAgilityPack and extract data from even the most complex HTML documents.

Chapter 6: Advanced Data Extraction Techniques

Introduction to Advanced Data Extraction Techniques

As data extraction grows in importance across industries, the complexity of web pages and the mechanisms used to display data present significant challenges. Modern web pages often feature dynamic content, nested structures, and interactive components, requiring advanced methods to retrieve the necessary information effectively. This chapter focuses on equipping readers with techniques to navigate and extract data from complex web environments, including the use of regular expressions and approaches to handle dynamic content.

6.1 Introduction to Selenium for Browser Automation in C#

Selenium is an essential library for automating web browsers. Although its primary use is in automated testing, it is incredibly effective for scraping websites with dynamic content rendered by JavaScript.

Setting Up Selenium in C#

Before you can start working with Selenium, you need to set up your environment:

1. **Install the Selenium WebDriver NuGet Package**
    - Open a terminal or command prompt in your project directory.
    - Run:

        dotnet add package Selenium.WebDriver

    - This command adds Selenium WebDriver to your project, enabling you to automate browser interactions.
2. **Download ChromeDriver**
    - Visit the official ChromeDriver website.
    - Download the version that matches your installed version of Chrome.
    - Extract it to a directory (e.g., C:\drivers).
3. **Add ChromeDriver to PATH**

- Add the directory containing the ChromeDriver executable to your system's PATH environment variable to simplify usage.

Example: Automating a Login Process

Here is an example program to automate logging into a website:

```
using OpenQA.Selenium;
using OpenQA.Selenium.Chrome;

class Program
{
    static void Main(string[] args)
    {
        // Set up the WebDriver
        IWebDriver driver = new ChromeDriver(@"C:\drivers"); // Ensure the path to ChromeDriver is correct.

        // Open the website
        driver.Navigate().GoToUrl("https://www.example.com/login");

        // Locate the username and password fields
        IWebElement username = driver.FindElement(By.Id("username")); // Find element by ID
        IWebElement password = driver.FindElement(By.Id("password"));

        // Input credentials
        username.SendKeys("your_username"); // Replace with your username
        password.SendKeys("your_password"); // Replace with your password

        // Submit the form
        password.SendKeys(Keys.Enter); // Simulate pressing 'Enter'

        // Close the browser after the task
        driver.Quit();
    }
}
```

Explanation of the Code:

- ChromeDriver: Initializes the WebDriver instance for Chrome.
- Navigate().GoToUrl: Opens the specified URL in the browser.
- FindElement: Locates elements on the page. Here, it uses the Id locator strategy to find fields for username and password.
- SendKeys: Simulates typing into input fields.
- Keys.Enter: Submits the form by simulating the 'Enter' key.
- Quit(): Closes the browser and cleans up resources.

6.2 Handling JavaScript-Rendered Content

Dynamic content is loaded asynchronously, often after the page's initial load. Using Selenium, you can wait for this content to load before extracting it.

Using Selenium to Wait for Content

Example: Scraping content that appears dynamically:

```csharp
using OpenQA.Selenium;
using OpenQA.Selenium.Chrome;
using OpenQA.Selenium.Support.UI;

class Program
{
    static void Main(string[] args)
    {
        // Set up the WebDriver
        IWebDriver driver = new ChromeDriver(@"C:\drivers");

        // Open the website
        driver.Navigate().GoToUrl("https://www.example.com");

        // Wait for the product list to load
        WebDriverWait wait = new WebDriverWait(driver, TimeSpan.FromSeconds(10));
        IWebElement element = wait.Until(ExpectedConditions.ElementIsVisible(By.Id("product-list")));

        // Extract and print the product list
        Console.WriteLine(element.Text);

        // Close the browser
        driver.Quit();
    }
}
```

Explanation of the Code:

- `WebDriverWait`: Provides an explicit wait mechanism, pausing the execution until a specified condition is met.
- `Until(ExpectedConditions.ElementIsVisible)`: Waits for an element with a specific ID (`product-list`) to be visible on the page.
- `ElementIsVisible`: A predefined condition to detect the presence of visible elements.

6.3 Interacting with Forms, Buttons, and Dropdowns

Selenium simplifies interactions with web elements like forms, buttons, and dropdowns.

Example: Filling and Submitting a Search Form

```csharp
using OpenQA.Selenium;
using OpenQA.Selenium.Chrome;
using OpenQA.Selenium.Support.UI;

class Program
{
    static void Main(string[] args)
```

```csharp
    {
        // Set up the WebDriver
        IWebDriver driver = new ChromeDriver(@"C:\drivers");

        // Open the website
        driver.Navigate().GoToUrl("https://www.example.com");

        // Fill out the search form
        IWebElement searchBox = driver.FindElement(By.Id("search-box"));
        searchBox.SendKeys("Web scraping tutorial");

        // Select a category
        IWebElement categoryDropdown = driver.FindElement(By.Id("category-dropdown"));
        SelectElement select = new SelectElement(categoryDropdown);
        select.SelectByText("Technology");

        // Submit the form
        searchBox.Submit();

        // Close the browser
        driver.Quit();
    }
}
```

Explanation of the Code:

- `SelectElement`: **Allows interaction with dropdown menus.**
- `SelectByText`: **Selects an option by its visible text.**
- `Submit`: **Submits the form.**

6.4 Handling Cookies and Sessions

Managing cookies and sessions ensures continuity across multiple interactions with a website.

Example: Getting, Setting, and Deleting Cookies

```csharp
using OpenQA.Selenium;
using OpenQA.Selenium.Chrome;

class Program
{
    static void Main(string[] args)
    {
        // Set up the WebDriver
        IWebDriver driver = new ChromeDriver(@"C:\drivers");

        // Open the website
        driver.Navigate().GoToUrl("https://www.example.com");

        // Get cookies
        var cookies = driver.Manage().Cookies.AllCookies;
        foreach (var cookie in cookies)
        {
```

```
                Console.WriteLine($"Cookie: {cookie.Name}, Value:
{cookie.Value}");
            }

        // Add a new cookie
        var newCookie = new Cookie("myCookie", "myValue");
        driver.Manage().Cookies.AddCookie(newCookie);

        // Delete all cookies
        driver.Manage().Cookies.DeleteAllCookies();

        // Close the browser
        driver.Quit();
    }
}
```

Explanation of the Code:

- `AllCookies`: **Retrieves all cookies from the current session.**
- `AddCookie`: **Adds a new cookie to the session.**
- `DeleteAllCookies`: **Clears all cookies for the session.**

6.5 Advanced Crawling with Asynchronous Tasks in C#

Asynchronous programming is essential when scraping multiple URLs to optimize time and resources. The provided code demonstrates how to use asynchronous tasks in C# to crawl multiple URLs in parallel using Selenium. The approach ensures efficient use of system resources while handling multiple browser instances.

Code:

```
public async Task CrawleIt()
{
    var Tasks = new List<Task>();
    var urls = System.IO.File.ReadAllLines("a2.txt"); // Read URLs from a file
    var browserCount = 7; // Number of browser instances
    var urlCount = urls.Length; // Total number of URLs
    var urlPerBrowser = urlCount / browserCount; // Number of URLs per browser

    for (int i = 0; i < browserCount; i++)
    {
        var counter = i;
        Tasks.Add(Task.Run(async () =>
        {
            ChromeOptions options = new ChromeOptions();
            options.AddArgument("--headless"); // Run in headless mode
            options.AddArgument("--disable-gpu"); // Disable GPU for headless mode
            ChromeDriver driver = new(options);
            driver.Navigate().GoToUrl($"{urls[counter]}");
            driver.Manage().Window.Maximize();
            LoadCookies(driver); // Load cookies into the browser

            try
```

```
            {
                for (int j = counter * browserCount; j < (counter *
browserCount) + urlPerBrowser; j++)
                {
                        driver.Navigate().GoToUrl($"{urls[j]}");

                        // Wait for the page to completely load
                        WebDriverWait wait = new WebDriverWait(driver,
TimeSpan.FromSeconds(5));

                        // Wait until the document.readyState is 'complete'
                        wait.Until(driver =>
((IJavaScriptExecutor)driver).ExecuteScript("return
document.readyState").Equals("complete"));

                        Thread.Sleep(TimeSpan.FromSeconds(3));

                        await
System.IO.File.WriteAllTextAsync(GetTelegramPhotoFileRootPath(_env,
$"file{GetUniqueId()}.html"), driver.PageSource);

                        Thread.Sleep(TimeSpan.FromSeconds(1));
                }
            }
            catch
            {
                // Handle any exceptions here
            }
            finally
            {
                driver?.Quit(); // Ensure browser closes even if an
exception occurs
                driver = null;
            }
        }));
    }

    await Task.WhenAll(Tasks); // Wait for all tasks to complete
    return View("index", "title");
}
```

Explanation of Each Line:

1. var Tasks = new List<Task>();
   - Initializes a list to store asynchronous tasks. Each task represents a browser instance handling a subset of URLs.
2. var urls = System.IO.File.ReadAllLines("a2.txt");
   - Reads all URLs from a file named a2.txt into an array. Each line in the file represents a URL.
3. var browserCount = 7;
   - Specifies the number of browser instances to run in parallel.
4. var urlCount = urls.Length;
   - Determines the total number of URLs to process.
5. var urlPerBrowser = urlCount / browserCount;
   - Calculates the number of URLs each browser instance will handle.
6. for (int i = 0; i < browserCount; i++)
   - Loops to create a task for each browser instance.

7. Tasks.Add(Task.Run(async () => { ... }));
   - Adds a new asynchronous task to the Tasks list. Each task operates independently.
8. ChromeOptions options = new ChromeOptions();
   - Configures ChromeDriver options.
9. options.AddArgument("--headless");
   - Runs the browser in headless mode, which is useful for scraping without opening a visible browser window.
10. driver.Navigate().GoToUrl($"{urls[counter]}");
    - Navigates the browser to the first URL assigned to this instance.
11. LoadCookies(driver);
    - A custom method (assumed) to load cookies into the browser, enabling authenticated requests.
12. for (int j = counter * browserCount; j < (counter * browserCount) + urlPerBrowser; j++)
    - Loops through the URLs assigned to this browser instance.
13. driver.Navigate().GoToUrl($"{urls[j]}");
    - Loads the next URL from the subset assigned to this browser instance.
14. WebDriverWait wait = new WebDriverWait(driver, TimeSpan.FromSeconds(5));
    - Sets up an explicit wait to ensure dynamic content is fully loaded.
15. wait.Until(driver => ((IJavaScriptExecutor)driver).ExecuteScript("return document.readyState").Equals("complete"));
    - Waits until the browser's document.readyState becomes "complete", indicating the page has fully loaded.
16. await System.IO.File.WriteAllTextAsync(GetTelegramPhotoFileRootPath(_env, $"file{GetUniqueId()}.html"), driver.PageSource);
    - Saves the page's HTML source to a file asynchronously. The file name includes a unique identifier.
17. Thread.Sleep(TimeSpan.FromSeconds(1));
    - Introduces a short delay between iterations to prevent overloading the target server.
18. driver?.Quit();
    - Closes the browser and releases resources.
19. await Task.WhenAll(Tasks);
    - Waits for all browser tasks to finish before proceeding.

Advice for Using This Code:

1. **Optimize Resource Allocation:**
   - Test with different browserCount values to avoid overloading your machine or the target server.
2. **Handle Errors Gracefully:**
   - Implement meaningful error-handling logic in the catch block to log issues and retry failed requests.
3. **Be Ethical and Legal:**
   - Ensure you have permission to scrape the target websites and respect their terms of service.
4. **Throttle Requests:**
   - Use appropriate delays and avoid sending too many requests in a short period.
5. **Secure Sensitive Data:**
   - If credentials or API keys are used, ensure they are stored securely and not hardcoded in the code.

6. **Test Scalability:**
   - Monitor memory and CPU usage when scaling up the number of tasks or URLs to prevent system overload.

Chapter Summary

In this chapter, we explored the use of Selenium for scraping dynamic websites, focusing on advanced techniques such as handling JavaScript-rendered content, interacting with forms, managing cookies, and parallelizing tasks using asynchronous programming.

The example of crawling multiple URLs with asynchronous tasks demonstrated how to efficiently utilize resources while handling complex web scraping scenarios.

By following best practices, such as ethical considerations, proper error handling, and resource management, developers can ensure robust and scalable scraping workflows.

Chapter 7. Working with APIs

APIs (Application Programming Interfaces) are the backbone of modern web applications and services, enabling seamless communication between different systems. This section will delve into the essentials of working with APIs in C#, offering a comprehensive guide on fetching data, handling authentication, utilizing third-party APIs, and overcoming common challenges. Let's explore these concepts in detail.

7.1 RESTful APIs and How They Work

REST (Representational State Transfer) APIs are widely used for building scalable and flexible web services. They leverage standard HTTP methods such as GET, POST, PUT, and DELETE to perform operations on resources identified by unique endpoints (URLs). Key topics include:

- **Difference Between RESTful and Non-RESTful APIs**
  RESTful APIs emphasize stateless communication, where each request contains all the information needed to process it, while non-RESTful APIs might rely on maintaining session states on the server.
- **HTTP Methods and Their Usage**
    - **GET**: Retrieve data from a server.
    - **POST**: Send data to a server to create resources.
    - **PUT**: Update existing resources or create new ones if they don't exist.
    - **DELETE**: Remove resources.

Here's a simple C# example of a RESTful API for a power bank store using ASP.NET Core. This implementation includes basic endpoints for managing power banks with the specified HTTP methods: GET, POST, PUT, and DELETE.

Steps:

1. Install ASP.NET Core SDK.
2. Create a new project (`dotnet new webapi`).
3. Add the following example code in the `Controllers` folder.

```csharp
using Microsoft.AspNetCore.Mvc;
using System.Collections.Generic;
using System.Linq;
```

```csharp
namespace PowerBankStore.Controllers
{
    [Route("api/[controller]")]
    [ApiController]
    public class PowerBanksController : ControllerBase
    {
        // Mock in-memory data store
        private static List<PowerBank> powerBanks = new List<PowerBank>
        {
            new PowerBank { Id = 1, Name = "FastCharge 10000mAh", Price = 29.99 },
            new PowerBank { Id = 2, Name = "UltraSlim 20000mAh", Price = 49.99 }
        };

        // GET: api/PowerBanks
        [HttpGet]
        public ActionResult<IEnumerable<PowerBank>> GetPowerBanks()
        {
            return Ok(powerBanks);
        }

        // GET: api/PowerBanks/{id}
        [HttpGet("{id}")]
        public ActionResult<PowerBank> GetPowerBank(int id)
        {
            var powerBank = powerBanks.FirstOrDefault(pb => pb.Id == id);
            if (powerBank == null)
            {
                return NotFound();
            }
            return Ok(powerBank);
        }

        // POST: api/PowerBanks
        [HttpPost]
        public ActionResult<PowerBank> CreatePowerBank([FromBody] PowerBank newPowerBank)
        {
            newPowerBank.Id = powerBanks.Count > 0 ? powerBanks.Max(pb => pb.Id) + 1 : 1;
            powerBanks.Add(newPowerBank);
            return CreatedAtAction(nameof(GetPowerBank), new { id = newPowerBank.Id }, newPowerBank);
        }

        // PUT: api/PowerBanks/{id}
        [HttpPut("{id}")]
        public IActionResult UpdatePowerBank(int id, [FromBody] PowerBank updatedPowerBank)
        {
            var powerBank = powerBanks.FirstOrDefault(pb => pb.Id == id);
            if (powerBank == null)
            {
                return NotFound();
            }

            powerBank.Name = updatedPowerBank.Name;
            powerBank.Price = updatedPowerBank.Price;
            return NoContent();
        }
```

```csharp
        // DELETE: api/PowerBanks/{id}
        [HttpDelete("{id}")]
        public IActionResult DeletePowerBank(int id)
        {
            var powerBank = powerBanks.FirstOrDefault(pb => pb.Id == id);
            if (powerBank == null)
            {
                return NotFound();
            }

            powerBanks.Remove(powerBank);
            return NoContent();
        }
    }

    // Model
    public class PowerBank
    {
        public int Id { get; set; }
        public string Name { get; set; }
        public double Price { get; set; }
    }
}
```

Explanation:

1. **GET**:
   - `/api/PowerBanks` - Retrieve all power banks.
   - `/api/PowerBanks/{id}` - Retrieve a specific power bank by ID.
2. **POST**:
   - `/api/PowerBanks` - Add a new power bank.
3. **PUT**:
   - `/api/PowerBanks/{id}` - Update an existing power bank or return 404 if not found.
4. **DELETE**:
   - `/api/PowerBanks/{id}` - Remove a power bank by ID.

Running the Code:

1. Start the API server (`dotnet run`).
2. Use a tool like **Postman** or **curl** to test the API endpoints.

- **API Endpoints and Resource Identification**
  Each resource in a RESTful API is identified by a unique URI. Examples include /users for all users and /users/{id} for a specific user.

To create a client application to consume the PowerBank API, you can use a C# Console App for simplicity. Below is an example client app that uses **HttpClient** to interact with the API endpoints.

Steps:

1. Create a new Console App project (`dotnet new console`).
2. Add the following code to the `Program.cs` file.

```csharp
using System;
using System.Collections.Generic;
using System.Net.Http;
using System.Net.Http.Json;
using System.Text;
using System.Text.Json;
using System.Threading.Tasks;

namespace PowerBankClient
{
    public class Program
    {
        private static readonly HttpClient client = new HttpClient { BaseAddress = new Uri("http://localhost:5000/api/PowerBanks") };

        public static async Task Main(string[] args)
        {
            Console.WriteLine("Power Bank Store Client");
            Console.WriteLine("=========================");

            while (true)
            {
                Console.WriteLine("\nChoose an option:");
                Console.WriteLine("1. Get all Power Banks");
                Console.WriteLine("2. Get Power Bank by ID");
                Console.WriteLine("3. Create a Power Bank");
                Console.WriteLine("4. Update a Power Bank");
                Console.WriteLine("5. Delete a Power Bank");
                Console.WriteLine("0. Exit");

                var choice = Console.ReadLine();
                switch (choice)
                {
                    case "1":
                        await GetAllPowerBanks();
                        break;
                    case "2":
                        await GetPowerBankById();
                        break;
                    case "3":
                        await CreatePowerBank();
                        break;
                    case "4":
                        await UpdatePowerBank();
                        break;
                    case "5":
                        await DeletePowerBank();
                        break;
                    case "0":
                        return;
                    default:
                        Console.WriteLine("Invalid option. Try again.");
                        break;
```

```csharp
            }
        }
    }

    private static async Task GetAllPowerBanks()
    {
        try
        {
            var powerBanks = await client.GetFromJsonAsync<List<PowerBank>>("");
            Console.WriteLine("\nPower Banks:");
            powerBanks.ForEach(pb => Console.WriteLine($"ID: {pb.Id}, Name: {pb.Name}, Price: ${pb.Price:F2}"));
        }
        catch (Exception ex)
        {
            Console.WriteLine($"Error: {ex.Message}");
        }
    }

    private static async Task GetPowerBankById()
    {
        Console.Write("Enter ID: ");
        var id = Console.ReadLine();
        try
        {
            var powerBank = await client.GetFromJsonAsync<PowerBank>($"/{id}");
            Console.WriteLine($"\nPower Bank - ID: {powerBank.Id}, Name: {powerBank.Name}, Price: ${powerBank.Price:F2}");
        }
        catch (Exception ex)
        {
            Console.WriteLine($"Error: {ex.Message}");
        }
    }

    private static async Task CreatePowerBank()
    {
        Console.Write("Enter Name: ");
        var name = Console.ReadLine();
        Console.Write("Enter Price: ");
        if (double.TryParse(Console.ReadLine(), out var price))
        {
            var newPowerBank = new PowerBank { Name = name, Price = price };
            var response = await client.PostAsJsonAsync("", newPowerBank);
            if (response.IsSuccessStatusCode)
            {
                Console.WriteLine("Power Bank created successfully.");
            }
            else
            {
                Console.WriteLine($"Error: {response.ReasonPhrase}");
            }
        }
        else
        {
            Console.WriteLine("Invalid price.");
        }
```

```csharp
        }

        private static async Task UpdatePowerBank()
        {
            Console.Write("Enter ID: ");
            var id = Console.ReadLine();
            Console.Write("Enter New Name: ");
            var name = Console.ReadLine();
            Console.Write("Enter New Price: ");
            if (double.TryParse(Console.ReadLine(), out var price))
            {
                var updatedPowerBank = new PowerBank { Name = name, Price = price };
                var response = await client.PutAsJsonAsync($"/{id}",
                    updatedPowerBank);
                if (response.IsSuccessStatusCode)
                {
                    Console.WriteLine("Power Bank updated successfully.");
                }
                else
                {
                    Console.WriteLine($"Error: {response.ReasonPhrase}");
                }
            }
            else
            {
                Console.WriteLine("Invalid price.");
            }
        }

        private static async Task DeletePowerBank()
        {
            Console.Write("Enter ID: ");
            var id = Console.ReadLine();
            var response = await client.DeleteAsync($"/{id}");
            if (response.IsSuccessStatusCode)
            {
                Console.WriteLine("Power Bank deleted successfully.");
            }
            else
            {
                Console.WriteLine($"Error: {response.ReasonPhrase}");
            }
        }
    }

    public class PowerBank
    {
        public int Id { get; set; }
        public string Name { get; set; }
        public double Price { get; set; }
    }
}
```

Explanation:

1. **Base Address**:
    - Replace http://localhost:5000/api/PowerBanks with the actual API URL (default for local ASP.NET Core API).
2. **Menu Options**:

- The app provides a menu for the user to choose actions like GET, POST, PUT, and DELETE.
3. **HttpClient**:
    - Makes requests to the API endpoints.
    - Uses methods like GetFromJsonAsync, PostAsJsonAsync, PutAsJsonAsync, and DeleteAsync to interact with the API.
4. **Error Handling**:
    - Includes basic error handling with try-catch.

Running the Client:

1. Start the PowerBank API server.
2. Run the console app (dotnet run).
3. Use the menu to interact with the API.

This is a straightforward example to get started. You can expand it with features like validation, logging, or user authentication.

7.2 Fetching and Parsing API Data in C#

Interacting with APIs in C# involves sending HTTP requests to a server and processing the returned data. This section dives deeper into essential techniques and considerations when working with APIs.

Using the HttpClient Class

The HttpClient class in .NET is the primary way to send HTTP requests and receive responses. It is versatile and supports GET, POST, PUT, DELETE, and other HTTP methods.

Example of fetching data with HttpClient:

```
using System;
using System.Net.Http;
using System.Threading.Tasks;

public class Program
{
    public static async Task Main(string[] args)
    {
        HttpClient client = new HttpClient();

        try
        {
            string url = "https://api.example.com/data";
            HttpResponseMessage response = await client.GetAsync(url);
```

```
            response.EnsureSuccessStatusCode(); // Throws exception for
non-success status codes

            string responseData = await
response.Content.ReadAsStringAsync();
            Console.WriteLine("Response Data:");
            Console.WriteLine(responseData);
        }
        catch (HttpRequestException ex)
        {
            Console.WriteLine($"Request error: {ex.Message}");
        }
        finally
        {
            client.Dispose(); // Dispose of HttpClient
        }
    }
}
```

Key Points:

- Use GetAsync, PostAsync, PutAsync, and DeleteAsync for specific HTTP methods.
- Call EnsureSuccessStatusCode() to throw exceptions for 4xx or 5xx responses.
- Always dispose of the HttpClient or use a using block to manage resources.

Parsing JSON and XML Data

Most APIs return data in JSON or XML formats. Parsing this data into objects in C# is straightforward with libraries like System.Text.Json and Newtonsoft.Json for JSON, and XmlSerializer for XML.

Parsing JSON with System.Text.Json:

```
using System;
using System.Net.Http;
using System.Text.Json;
using System.Threading.Tasks;

public class Program
{
    public static async Task Main(string[] args)
    {
        HttpClient client = new HttpClient();

        try
        {
            string url = "https://api.example.com/data";
            string responseData = await client.GetStringAsync(url);

            var myData = JsonSerializer.Deserialize<MyData>(responseData);
            Console.WriteLine($"Name: {myData.Name}, Age: {myData.Age}");
        }
        catch (Exception ex)
        {
```

```
            Console.WriteLine($"Error: {ex.Message}");
        }
    }

    public class MyData
    {
        public string Name { get; set; }
        public int Age { get; set; }
    }
}
```

Parsing XML with XmlSerializer:

```
using System;
using System.IO;
using System.Net.Http;
using System.Xml.Serialization;

public class Program
{
    public static async Task Main(string[] args)
    {
        HttpClient client = new HttpClient();

        try
        {
            string url = "https://api.example.com/data.xml";
            string responseData = await client.GetStringAsync(url);

            var serializer = new XmlSerializer(typeof(MyData));
            using (StringReader reader = new StringReader(responseData))
            {
                var myData = (MyData)serializer.Deserialize(reader);
                Console.WriteLine($"Name: {myData.Name}, Age: {myData.Age}");
            }
        }
        catch (Exception ex)
        {
            Console.WriteLine($"Error: {ex.Message}");
        }
    }

    [XmlRoot("Data")]
    public class MyData
    {
        public string Name { get; set; }
        public int Age { get; set; }
    }
}
```

Handling Errors and Exceptions

Network communication can be unpredictable, so it's important to handle errors gracefully.

Common scenarios to handle:

- **Network timeouts**: Catch TaskCanceledException or set a timeout on HttpClient.
- **Invalid responses**: Check response status codes and validate the content.
- **Server errors**: Implement retry mechanisms.

Example of robust error handling:

```
try
{
    HttpResponseMessage response = await client.GetAsync("https://api.example.com/data");
    response.EnsureSuccessStatusCode();

    string responseData = await response.Content.ReadAsStringAsync();
}
catch (HttpRequestException ex)
{
    Console.WriteLine($"HTTP Request error: {ex.Message}");
}
catch (TaskCanceledException)
{
    Console.WriteLine("Request timeout. Please try again.");
}
catch (Exception ex)
{
    Console.WriteLine($"Unexpected error: {ex.Message}");
}
```

Implementing Caching and Retries

To improve performance and reliability, implement caching and retries using tools like MemoryCache or Polly.

Example: In-Memory Caching:

```
using Microsoft.Extensions.Caching.Memory;
using System;

public class Program
{
    private static readonly MemoryCache cache = new MemoryCache(new MemoryCacheOptions());

    public static string GetData(string key)
    {
        if (cache.TryGetValue(key, out string cachedData))
        {
            return cachedData;
        }

        // Simulate data fetching
        string newData = "Fetched Data";
        cache.Set(key, newData, TimeSpan.FromMinutes(5));
        return newData;
```

        }
}

Example: Retry with Polly:

```
using Polly;
using Polly.Retry;
using System;
using System.Net.Http;
using System.Threading.Tasks;

public class Program
{
    public static async Task Main(string[] args)
    {
        HttpClient client = new HttpClient();
        AsyncRetryPolicy retryPolicy = Policy
            .Handle<HttpRequestException>()
            .WaitAndRetryAsync(3, retryAttempt => TimeSpan.FromSeconds(retryAttempt));

        await retryPolicy.ExecuteAsync(async () =>
        {
            HttpResponseMessage response = await client.GetAsync("https://api.example.com/data");
            response.EnsureSuccessStatusCode();
            string responseData = await response.Content.ReadAsStringAsync();
            Console.WriteLine(responseData);
        });
    }
}
```

By combining these techniques—HttpClient, parsing libraries, error handling, caching, and retries—you can build robust C# applications that reliably interact with APIs.

7.3 Managing Authentication for APIs

Authentication ensures secure access to API resources. Learn about:

- **API Keys**
  Simple tokens passed in headers or query strings. Store them securely, e.g., in environment variables.
- **OAuth 2.0 and OpenID Connect**
  Standard protocols for secure, token-based authentication. Implement flows like Authorization Code Grant.
- **Basic and Digest Authentication**
  Use encoded credentials in headers for Basic authentication, or hashed credentials for Digest.

- **JSON Web Tokens (JWTs)**
  Self-contained tokens used for both authentication and authorization.

7.4 Using Third-Party APIs for Web Scraping

Web scraping extracts data from web pages. Topics include:

- **Introduction to Web Scraping**
  Applications include data aggregation, competitor analysis, and market research.
- **Popular Web Scraping Tools**
  - **Beautiful Soup**: Python library for parsing HTML and XML.
  - **Scrapy**: Python-based framework for advanced scraping tasks.
  - **Selenium**: Browser automation tool for dynamic web pages.
- **Third-Party APIs**
  - **Google Custom Search API**: Retrieve search results programmatically.
  - **Bing Web Search API**: Similar to Google's API, offering data extraction capabilities.
  - **Amazon Product Advertising API**: Access Amazon product details for e-commerce applications.
- **Handling Anti-Scraping Measures**
  Use techniques like IP rotation, delays, and respecting robots.txt files to avoid detection.

7.5 Advanced Topics in API Integration

- **API Gateway:**

  - **Description:** An intermediary server that acts as a single entry point for all API requests.

  - **Benefits:**

    - **Centralized Management:** Manage all your APIs from a single point, making it easier to control access, enforce security policies, and monitor usage.

    - **Traffic Management:** Route requests to the appropriate backend services, handle load balancing, and implement rate limiting.

    - **Security:** Enforce authentication, authorization, and data encryption at the gateway level.

  - **Examples:**

    - **Azure API Management:** A fully managed service for publishing, securing, transforming, and monitoring APIs.

- **AWS API Gateway:** A fully managed service that makes it easy for developers to create, publish, maintain, monitor, and secure APIs at any scale. [1]

1. www.astronomer.io

www.astronomer.io

- Service Discovery and Load Balancing:
    - **Description:** Mechanisms that help applications dynamically locate and interact with other services within a microservices architecture.
    - Benefits:
        - **Dynamic Routing:** Automatically route requests to available instances of a service, even if the number of instances changes.
        - **Load Balancing:** Distribute traffic evenly across multiple instances of a service to improve performance and availability.
        - **Fault Tolerance:** Isolate failures and prevent cascading failures within the system.
    - Examples:
        - **Consul:** A service mesh that provides service discovery, health checks, and more.
        - **Eureka:** A service registry for Netflix that allows applications to dynamically discover other services in the same virtual datacenter.
- Caching and CDNs:
    - Description:
        - **Caching:** Storing frequently accessed data in memory or on disk to reduce the need to repeatedly fetch it from the source.
        - **CDN (Content Delivery Network):** A distributed network of servers that deliver content to users based on their geographic location.
    - Benefits:
        - **Improved Performance:** Reduce latency and improve response times by serving cached data or content from a nearby server.

- **Reduced Load on Origin Servers:** Offload traffic from the origin servers, improving their scalability and availability.
- **Cost Savings:** Reduce bandwidth costs by serving cached content.
  - Example:
    - **Redis:** An in-memory data store often used for caching.
    - **Cloudflare, Fastly:** Popular CDN providers.
- **Message Queues and Streaming:**
  - **Description:** Technologies that enable asynchronous communication between applications.
  - Benefits:
    - **Decoupling:** Loosely couple applications, allowing them to operate independently.
    - **Scalability:** Handle high volumes of messages and events efficiently.
    - **Real-time Processing:** Enable real-time data processing and stream processing applications.
  - Examples:
    - **Kafka:** A high-throughput, distributed streaming platform.
    - **RabbitMQ:** A popular message broker that supports various messaging patterns.
- **Security Considerations:**
  - **Encryption (TLS):** Encrypt data in transit to protect it from eavesdropping.
  - **Role-Based Access Control (RBAC):** Grant different levels of access to different users or applications based on their roles.
  - **API Keys and Authentication:** Implement secure authentication mechanisms to verify the identity of clients.
  - **Regular Security Audits:** Conduct regular security assessments to identify and address vulnerabilities.

7.6 Troubleshooting and Debugging API Issues

Debugging Tools:
- **Postman:** A popular tool for testing APIs, sending requests, and inspecting responses.
- **Fiddler:** A web debugging proxy that captures and inspects HTTP traffic.

- Wireshark: A network protocol analyzer that allows you to inspect network packets.

Logging and Monitoring:
- Logging: Log all API requests and responses, including timestamps, request parameters, response codes, and any errors.
- Monitoring: Use monitoring tools to track API performance metrics, such as response times, error rates, and traffic volume.
- Examples:
  - Application Insights: A cloud-based application performance management service from Microsoft.
  - ELK Stack (Elasticsearch, Logstash, Kibana): A popular open-source platform for collecting, analyzing, and visualizing log data.

Handling API Errors:
- HTTP Status Codes: Understand the meaning of different HTTP status codes (e.g., 404 Not Found, 500 Internal Server Error) to diagnose and handle errors effectively.
- Error Handling Mechanisms: Implement robust error handling mechanisms to gracefully handle unexpected situations and provide informative error messages to clients.

Important Error Codes and Explanations in API Integration

4xx Client Errors

400 Bad Request:
- Explanation: The server cannot process the request due to invalid syntax, missing parameters, or invalid data.
- Example: Sending a request with the wrong data type for a parameter.

- **401 Unauthorized:**
  - Explanation: The request requires user authentication or the provided credentials are invalid.
  - Example: Missing or incorrect API key, invalid username/password.

- **403 Forbidden:**
  - Explanation: The server understands the request but refuses to authorize it.
  - Example: Insufficient permissions to access the requested resource, rate limiting exceeded.

- **404 Not Found:**

- o **Explanation:** The requested resource (e.g., a specific endpoint or data) could not be found on the server.
- o **Example:** Requesting a non-existent URL or a deleted resource.

- 422 Unprocessable Entity:
  - o **Explanation:** The server understands the content type of the request entity, and the syntax of the request entity is correct, but it was unable to process the contained instructions. [1]

1. blog.rabiaqadeer.se

blog.rabiaqadeer.se

- o **Example:** Data validation errors, missing required fields in the request body.

5xx Server Errors

500 Internal Server Error:
- o **Explanation:** A generic error indicating that the server encountered an unexpected condition that prevented it from fulfilling the request.
- o **Example:** Server-side bugs, database errors, resource exhaustion.

- 502 Bad Gateway:
  - o **Explanation:** The server received an invalid response from an upstream server it accessed to fulfill the request.
  - o **Example:** Problems with a backend service or network connectivity issues.

- 503 Service Unavailable:
  - o **Explanation:** The server is currently unavailable (overloaded or down for maintenance).
  - o **Example:** Server overload, scheduled maintenance.

Key Considerations:

- **Error Handling:** Implement robust error handling on both the client and server sides to gracefully handle these errors and provide informative feedback to users.
- **Error Responses:** Include detailed error messages in the API responses to help developers diagnose and resolve issues.

- **Error Logging:** Log all errors, including the error code, timestamp, request details, and any relevant stack traces, for debugging and analysis.

    By understanding these common error codes and implementing proper error handling mechanisms, you can build more reliable and user-friendly APIs.

Best Practices for Debugging:
- o **Simulate Scenarios:** Test APIs with different input parameters and under various conditions to identify potential issues.
- o **Validate Data Integrity:** Ensure that data is being transmitted and processed correctly.
- o **Systematic Approach:** Use a structured approach to debugging, such as isolating the problem, forming hypotheses, and testing them systematically.

Code Example by implementing Error Handling and HTTP Error codes:

```
using System;

using System.Net.Http;

using System.Net.Http.Headers;

using System.Threading.Tasks;

using Microsoft.Extensions.Logging;

using Newtonsoft.Json;


public class JobBoardApiClient
{
  private readonly HttpClient _httpClient;
  private readonly ILogger<JobBoardApiClient> _logger;


  public JobBoardApiClient(HttpClient httpClient, ILogger<JobBoardApiClient> logger)
  {
    _httpClient = httpClient;
    _logger = logger;


    // Configure HttpClient (optional)
    _httpClient.DefaultRequestHeaders.Accept.Clear();
```

```csharp
    _httpClient.DefaultRequestHeaders.Accept.Add(new MediaTypeWithQualityHeaderValue("application/json"));
}


public async Task<T> GetAsync<T>(string endpoint)
{
    try
    {
        HttpResponseMessage response = await _httpClient.GetAsync(endpoint);

        if (response.IsSuccessStatusCode)
        {
            string content = await response.Content.ReadAsStringAsync();
            return JsonConvert.DeserializeObject<T>(content);
        }
        else
        {
            _logger.LogError($"API request failed. Endpoint: {endpoint}, Status Code: {(int)response.StatusCode}, Reason: {response.ReasonPhrase}");
            HandleApiError(response);
            throw new HttpRequestException($"API request failed. Status Code: {(int)response.StatusCode}, Reason: {response.ReasonPhrase}");
        }
    }
    catch (Exception ex)
    {
        _logger.LogError($"An error occurred while making the API request to {endpoint}. Exception: {ex.Message}");
        throw; // Re-throw the exception for higher-level handling
    }
}
```

```csharp
        private void HandleApiError(HttpResponseMessage response)
        {
            // Handle specific error codes here, e.g.,
            switch ((int)response.StatusCode)
            {
                case 401:
                    // Handle authentication/authorization errors
                    _logger.LogWarning("Unauthorized access to the API.");
                    break;
                case 404:
                    // Handle resource not found
                    _logger.LogWarning($"Resource not found at {response.RequestMessage.RequestUri}");
                    break;
                case 500:
                    // Handle server errors
                    _logger.LogError("Internal server error encountered.");
                    break;
                // Handle other error codes as needed
            }
        }
    }
```

Explanation:

1. **Constructor:**
    - Initializes the HttpClient and ILogger properties.
    - Configures the HttpClient with the desired headers (e.g., Accept header for JSON).

2. **GetAsync Method:**
    - Makes an asynchronous GET request to the specified endpoint.

- Checks the IsSuccessStatusCode of the response.
    - If successful, deserializes the JSON response content into the specified type T using JsonConvert.DeserializeObject<T>().
    - If unsuccessful:
        - Logs the error with details (endpoint, status code, reason phrase) using _logger.LogError().
        - Calls the HandleApiError method to handle specific error codes.
        - Throws an HttpRequestException to propagate the error.
- Includes a general catch block to handle any unexpected exceptions that might occur during the request.

3. **HandleApiError Method:**
    - This method can be extended to handle specific error codes differently based on the needs of your application.
    - Currently, it includes basic handling for 401 (Unauthorized), 404 (Not Found), and 500 (Internal Server Error).

Key Improvements:

- **Error Logging:** Logs detailed error information (endpoint, status code, reason phrase) for easier debugging and troubleshooting.
- **Specific Error Handling:** The HandleApiError method allows for customized handling of different error codes.
- **Exception Handling:** Includes a general catch block to handle unexpected exceptions and prevent the application from crashing.
- **Dependency Injection:** The HttpClient and ILogger are injected into the constructor, making the class more testable and easier to maintain.

Usage Example:

C#

```csharp
// In your service or controller

public async Task<JobSearchResult> GetJobsByKeywordAsync(string keyword)
{
    string endpoint = $"/api/jobs?keyword={keyword}";
    JobSearchResult result = await _jobBoardApiClient.GetAsync<JobSearchResult>(endpoint);
    return result;
```

}

Note:

- This is a basic example, and you may need to adapt it further based on the specific requirements of your job board API and application.

- Consider implementing more advanced error handling strategies, such as retry mechanisms, circuit breakers, or custom exception classes.

This code provides a solid foundation for handling errors and logging in your C# API integration with a job board site. Remember to adapt it to your specific needs and best practices.

By mastering these aspects, developers can effectively harness the power of APIs, enabling seamless integration and data exchange across diverse systems.

Chapter 8. Data Storage and Export

In this chapter, we will delve into the crucial aspect of data storage and export, which is essential for any data-driven application. We will explore the various ways to save and manage data, including CSV, JSON, and databases. Additionally, we will introduce two popular database management systems, SQL Server and SQLite, and discuss how to use Entity Framework for efficient data handling.

Importance of Saving Data

Data storage is a cornerstone of modern applications, enabling the preservation, retrieval, and manipulation of information essential for functionality and decision-making. Properly saving data ensures reliability, enhances performance, supports scalability, and allows seamless integration with other systems. A robust data storage strategy also facilitates compliance with legal and regulatory requirements for data handling.

This chapter explores various methods of saving and managing data, emphasizing their practical applications. We will delve into commonly used formats like CSV and JSON, as well as database solutions such as SQL Server and SQLite. Additionally, we will cover Entity Framework as a tool for efficient data handling in .NET applications.

8.1 Saving Data to CSV, JSON, and Databases

CSV (Comma-Separated Values)

CSV files store tabular data in plain text, making them ideal for lightweight and straightforward data exchange. Below is an example of how to scrape data from a glass story website and save it as a CSV file in C#:

using System;

using System.Collections.Generic;

using System.IO;

using System.Net.Http;

using System.Threading.Tasks;

using HtmlAgilityPack;

```csharp
class Program
{
    static async Task Main()
    {
        string url = "https://www.glassstory.com/";

        using (HttpClient client = new HttpClient())
        {
            HttpResponseMessage response = await client.GetAsync(url);

            if (response.IsSuccessStatusCode)
            {
                string html = await response.Content.ReadAsStringAsync();
                HtmlDocument doc = new HtmlDocument();
                doc.LoadHtml(html);

                List<GlassStory> glassStories = new List<GlassStory>();
                foreach (HtmlNode node in doc.DocumentNode.SelectNodes("//div[@class='glass-story']"))
                {
                    GlassStory story = new GlassStory
                    {
                        Title = node.SelectSingleNode(".//h2[@class='title']").InnerText,
                        Description = node.SelectSingleNode(".//p[@class='description']").InnerText,
                        ImageUrl = node.SelectSingleNode(".//img[@class='image']").GetAttributeValue("src", "")
                    };
                    glassStories.Add(story);
                }

                using (StreamWriter writer = new StreamWriter("glass-stories.csv"))
```

```csharp
        {
            writer.WriteLine("Title,Description,ImageUrl");
            foreach (GlassStory story in glassStories)
            {
                writer.WriteLine($"{story.Title},{story.Description},{story.ImageUrl}");
            }
        }
      }
    }
}

public class GlassStory
{
    public string Title { get; set; }
    public string Description { get; set; }
    public string ImageUrl { get; set; }
}
```

JSON (JavaScript Object Notation)

JSON is a lightweight format for storing and transporting data, widely used for web applications and APIs. Here's an example to save scraped data in JSON format:

```csharp
using System;
using System.Collections.Generic;
using System.IO;
using System.Net.Http;
using System.Text.Json;
using System.Threading.Tasks;
using HtmlAgilityPack;


class Program
{
    static async Task Main()
```

```csharp
{
    string url = "https://www.glassstory.com/";

    using (HttpClient client = new HttpClient())
    {
        HttpResponseMessage response = await client.GetAsync(url);

        if (response.IsSuccessStatusCode)
        {
            string html = await response.Content.ReadAsStringAsync();
            HtmlDocument doc = new HtmlDocument();
            doc.LoadHtml(html);

            List<GlassStory> glassStories = new List<GlassStory>();
            foreach (HtmlNode node in doc.DocumentNode.SelectNodes("//div[@class='glass-story']"))
            {
                GlassStory story = new GlassStory
                {
                    Title = node.SelectSingleNode(".//h2[@class='title']").InnerText,
                    Description = node.SelectSingleNode(".//p[@class='description']").InnerText,
                    ImageUrl = node.SelectSingleNode(".//img[@class='image']").GetAttributeValue("src", "")
                };
                glassStories.Add(story);
            }

            string json = JsonSerializer.Serialize(glassStories);
            File.WriteAllText("glass-stories.json", json);
        }
    }
}
```

}

```csharp
public class GlassStory
{
    public string Title { get; set; }
    public string Description { get; set; }
    public string ImageUrl { get; set; }
}
```

Databases

Databases provide structured storage for data, supporting complex queries and efficient manipulation. Below is an example of saving data to a SQL Server database:

```csharp
using System;
using System.Collections.Generic;
using System.Data.SqlClient;
using System.Net.Http;
using System.Threading.Tasks;
using HtmlAgilityPack;

class Program
{
    static async Task Main()
    {
        string url = "https://www.glassstory.com/";

        using (HttpClient client = new HttpClient())
        {
            HttpResponseMessage response = await client.GetAsync(url);

            if (response.IsSuccessStatusCode)
            {
                string html = await response.Content.ReadAsStringAsync();
                HtmlDocument doc = new HtmlDocument();
```

```csharp
            doc.LoadHtml(html);

            List<GlassStory> glassStories = new List<GlassStory>();
            foreach (HtmlNode node in doc.DocumentNode.SelectNodes("//div[@class='glass-story']"))
            {
                GlassStory story = new GlassStory
                {
                    Title = node.SelectSingleNode(".//h2[@class='title']").InnerText,
                    Description = node.SelectSingleNode(".//p[@class='description']").InnerText,
                    ImageUrl = node.SelectSingleNode(".//img[@class='image']").GetAttributeValue("src", "")
                };
                glassStories.Add(story);
            }

            using (SqlConnection connection = new SqlConnection("Server=myServer;Database=myDatabase;User Id=myUser;Password=myPassword;"))
            {
                connection.Open();

                foreach (GlassStory story in glassStories)
                {
                    using (SqlCommand command = new SqlCommand("INSERT INTO GlassStories (Title, Description, ImageUrl) VALUES (@Title, @Description, @ImageUrl)", connection))
                    {
                        command.Parameters.AddWithValue("@Title", story.Title);
                        command.Parameters.AddWithValue("@Description", story.Description);
                        command.Parameters.AddWithValue("@ImageUrl", story.ImageUrl);
                        command.ExecuteNonQuery();
                    }
                }
```

```
        }
      }
    }
  }
}


public class GlassStory
{
    public string Title { get; set; }
    public string Description { get; set; }
    public string ImageUrl { get; set; }
}
```

8.2 Introduction to SQL Server and SQLite

SQL Server

SQL Server is a robust and scalable relational database management system developed by Microsoft. Below is an example of creating a database and table in SQL Server using T-SQL:

```
CREATE DATABASE GlassStories;
GO


USE GlassStories;
GO


CREATE TABLE GlassStories (
    Id INT PRIMARY KEY IDENTITY(1,1),
    Title NVARCHAR(100),
    Description NVARCHAR(500),
    ImageUrl NVARCHAR(300)
);
GO
```

SQLite

SQLite is a lightweight, file-based database engine. Here's an example of creating a table in SQLite:

```sql
CREATE TABLE GlassStories (
    Id INTEGER PRIMARY KEY AUTOINCREMENT,
    Title TEXT,
    Description TEXT,
    ImageUrl TEXT
);
```

8.3 Using Entity Framework for Data Handling

Database-First Approach

Entity Framework can generate .NET classes from an existing database schema. Here's an example of querying a database using the database-first approach:

```csharp
using System;
using System.Linq;

class Program
{
    static void Main()
    {
        using (GlassStoriesDbContext context = new GlassStoriesDbContext())
        {
            var glassStories = context.GlassStories.ToList();

            foreach (var story in glassStories)
            {
                Console.WriteLine(story.Title);
            }
        }
    }
}

public class GlassStoriesDbContext : DbContext
{
```

```csharp
    public DbSet<GlassStory> GlassStories { get; set; }
}


public class GlassStory
{
    public int Id { get; set; }
    public string Title { get; set; }
    public string Description { get; set; }
    public string ImageUrl { get; set; }
}
```

Code-First Approach

The code-first approach allows developers to define data models as .NET classes and generate the database schema from them. Below is an example:

```csharp
using System;
using System.Linq;

class Program
{
    static void Main()
    {
        using (GlassStoriesDbContext context = new GlassStoriesDbContext())
        {
            context.GlassStories.Add(new GlassStory
            {
                Title = "New Glass Story",
                Description = "This is a new glass story.",
                ImageUrl = "https://example.com/image.jpg"
            });

            context.SaveChanges();
        }
    }
}
```

```csharp
}

public class GlassStoriesDbContext : DbContext
{
    public DbSet<GlassStory> GlassStories { get; set; }
}

public class GlassStory
{
    public int Id { get; set; }
    public string Title { get; set; }
    public string Description { get; set; }
    public string ImageUrl { get; set; }
}
```

CRUD (Create, Read, Update, Delete) operations using the provided GlassStoriesDbContext and GlassStory classes in C# with Entity Framework Core:

1. Create

C#

```csharp
using (var context = new GlassStoriesDbContext())
{
    var newStory = new GlassStory
    {
        Title = "A Tale of Crystal",
        Description = "A captivating story about a glassblower...",
        ImageUrl = "path/to/image.jpg"
    };

    context.GlassStories.Add(newStory);
    context.SaveChanges();
}
```

2. Read (Get All)

C#

```csharp
using (var context = new GlassStoriesDbContext())
{
    var allStories = context.GlassStories.ToList();

    foreach (var story in allStories)
    {
        Console.WriteLine($"Title: {story.Title}");
        Console.WriteLine($"Description: {story.Description}");
        Console.WriteLine($"Image URL: {story.ImageUrl}");
        Console.WriteLine("-----");
    }
}
```

3. Read (Get By Id)

C#

```csharp
using (var context = new GlassStoriesDbContext())
{
    int storyId = 1; // Replace with the desired ID
    var story = context.GlassStories.FirstOrDefault(s => s.Id == storyId);

    if (story != null)
    {
        Console.WriteLine($"Title: {story.Title}");
        Console.WriteLine($"Description: {story.Description}");
        Console.WriteLine($"Image URL: {story.ImageUrl}");
    }
    else
    {
        Console.WriteLine("Story not found.");
    }
}
```

4. Update
C#

using (var context = new GlassStoriesDbContext())
{
   int storyId = 1; // Replace with the ID of the story to update

   var storyToUpdate = context.GlassStories.FirstOrDefault(s => s.Id == storyId);

   if (storyToUpdate != null)
   {
     storyToUpdate.Title = "Updated Title";

     storyToUpdate.Description = "Updated Description";

     storyToUpdate.ImageUrl = "path/to/new/image.jpg";

     context.SaveChanges();
   }
}

5. Delete
C#

using (var context = new GlassStoriesDbContext())
{
   int storyId = 1; // Replace with the ID of the story to delete

   var storyToDelete = context.GlassStories.FirstOrDefault(s => s.Id == storyId);

   if (storyToDelete != null)
   {
     context.GlassStories.Remove(storyToDelete);

     context.SaveChanges();
   }
}

Key Considerations:

- **Error Handling:** The provided examples are basic. In a real-world application, you'd want to add robust error handling (e.g., try-catch blocks) to gracefully handle potential exceptions (e.g., database connection issues, invalid IDs).
- **Data Validation:** Implement data validation to ensure that the data entered for each property of the GlassStory class is valid (e.g., non-empty strings, valid image URLs).
- **Security:** If you're working with sensitive data, consider implementing appropriate security measures to prevent unauthorized access and data breaches.
- **Asynchronous Operations:** For improved performance, especially with larger datasets, consider using asynchronous methods (e.g., await and async) for database operations.

This example provides a basic foundation for CRUD operations. You can further enhance it by adding features like filtering, sorting, pagination, and more complex query logic.

Chapter 9. Deploying and Automating Your Scraper

9.1: Introduction to Deploying and Automating Your Scraper

Deploying and automating your web scraper is a crucial step in making it a reliable and efficient tool. After building and testing your scraper, you need to deploy it to a production environment where it can run automatically without manual intervention. This not only saves time but also ensures that your scraper runs consistently and captures the required data.

One of the key aspects of deploying and automating your scraper is scheduling tasks. This involves setting up a schedule to run your scraper at specific intervals, such as daily, weekly, or monthly, depending on your requirements. This ensures that your scraper runs automatically and captures the required data at the scheduled times.

There are several tools and technologies available for scheduling tasks, including ASP.NET Task Scheduler. In this section, we will explore how to use ASP.NET Task Scheduler to schedule tasks for your web scraper.

1. Understanding Deployment Needs

Hosting Environment: Ensure your hosting setup supports ASP.NET (e.g., a Windows Server with IIS or a compatible cloud platform). Your host must have adequate resources for running the scraper (CPU, RAM, and network bandwidth).

Database and Storage: Determine where you will store the scraped data (e.g., SQL Server, Azure Storage, or a file system).

Code Packaging: Package your scraper as a runnable application, such as an ASP.NET Core Web API or a background service.

2. Automation and Scheduling

Task Scheduling in ASP.NET: ASP.NET does not include a built-in task scheduler by default, but you can achieve scheduling using libraries or external tools:

Quartz.NET: A powerful library for scheduling background jobs in .NET.

Hangfire: Another popular option for background task processing.

Alternatively, you can use Windows Task Scheduler or cron jobs on your server to trigger the scraper application at defined intervals.

ASP.NET Task Scheduler: If you prefer a lightweight solution, you can integrate task scheduling directly into your ASP.NET project using hosted services. In ASP.NET Core, this is done by implementing IHostedService.

3. Implementing Automation

Setting Up a Timer Service: If using ASP.NET Core, create a TimerHostedService to periodically trigger your scraping logic.

Here's an example of an **ASP.NET Core** application that implements a background service to fetch data from a flight website and save it to an **EF Core in-memory database**.

Steps Overview:

1. **Create a new ASP.NET Core project.**
2. **Add an Entity Framework Core in-memory database.**
3. **Implement a BackgroundService to fetch flight data periodically.**
4. **Create a controller to display the fetched flight data.**

Full Example Code

1. Install Required NuGet Packages

Run these commands in the Package Manager Console or add them via the NuGet Manager:

bash

```
dotnet add package Microsoft.EntityFrameworkCore.InMemory
dotnet add package Microsoft.AspNetCore.Http.Json
```

2. Define the Flight Model

```csharp
public class Flight
{
    public int Id { get; set; }
    public string Airline { get; set; }
    public string FlightNumber { get; set; }
    public string Origin { get; set; }
    public string Destination { get; set; }
    public DateTime DepartureTime { get; set; }
    public DateTime ArrivalTime { get; set; }
}
```

3. Create the EF Core DbContext

```csharp
using Microsoft.EntityFrameworkCore;

public class FlightDbContext : DbContext
{
    public DbSet<Flight> Flights { get; set; }

    public FlightDbContext(DbContextOptions<FlightDbContext> options) : base(options) { }
}
```

4. Implement the Background Service

```csharp
using System.Net.Http.Json;
using Microsoft.Extensions.Hosting;
```

```csharp
public class FlightDataFetcherService : BackgroundService
{
    private readonly IServiceProvider _serviceProvider;
    private readonly HttpClient _httpClient;

    public FlightDataFetcherService(IServiceProvider serviceProvider)
    {
        _serviceProvider = serviceProvider;
        _httpClient = new HttpClient();
    }

    protected override async Task ExecuteAsync(CancellationToken stoppingToken)
    {
        while (!stoppingToken.IsCancellationRequested)
        {
            await FetchAndSaveFlightDataAsync();
            await Task.Delay(TimeSpan.FromMinutes(5), stoppingToken); // Run every 5 minutes
        }
    }

    private async Task FetchAndSaveFlightDataAsync()
    {
        // Simulate fetching flight data
        var flightData = await _httpClient.GetFromJsonAsync<List<Flight>>("https://example.com/api/flights");

        if (flightData != null)
        {
            using var scope = _serviceProvider.CreateScope();
            var dbContext = scope.ServiceProvider.GetRequiredService<FlightDbContext>();
```

```csharp
            dbContext.Flights.RemoveRange(dbContext.Flights); // Clear old data
            dbContext.Flights.AddRange(flightData);        // Save new data
            await dbContext.SaveChangesAsync();
        }
    }
}
```

5. Register Services in Program.cs

```csharp
using Microsoft.EntityFrameworkCore;

var builder = WebApplication.CreateBuilder(args);

// Add DbContext with in-memory database
builder.Services.AddDbContext<FlightDbContext>(options =>
    options.UseInMemoryDatabase("FlightDB"));

// Register Background Service
builder.Services.AddHostedService<FlightDataFetcherService>();

// Add Controllers
builder.Services.AddControllers();

var app = builder.Build();

// Map Controllers
app.MapControllers();

app.Run();
```

6. Create a Controller to Access Flight Data

```csharp
using Microsoft.AspNetCore.Mvc;

[ApiController]
[Route("api/[controller]")]
public class FlightsController : ControllerBase
{
    private readonly FlightDbContext _dbContext;

    public FlightsController(FlightDbContext dbContext)
    {
        _dbContext = dbContext;
    }

    [HttpGet]
    public IActionResult GetFlights()
    {
        var flights = _dbContext.Flights.ToList();
        return Ok(flights);
    }
}
```

7. Run the Application

- Start the application: dotnet run.
- Access flight data via the API: http://localhost:5000/api/flights.

Sample Response

If https://example.com/api/flights returns:

json

[

```
  {
    "id": 1,
    "airline": "Airline A",
    "flightNumber": "AA123",
    "origin": "LAX",
    "destination": "JFK",
    "departureTime": "2024-12-28T08:00:00",
    "arrivalTime": "2024-12-28T14:00:00"
  }
]
```

Then, calling the GET /api/flights endpoint will return the same data saved in the in-memory database.

This setup simulates fetching and persisting data with an in-memory database, suitable for development or testing purposes. For production, replace the in-memory database with a persistent one like SQL Server.

Use third-party cloud tools (e.g., Azure Logic Apps or AWS Lambda) for scalability.

4. Steps to Deploy

Build the Project: Ensure the scraper project is optimized and compiled for production (release mode).

Configure Hosting: Deploy the scraper to your host using:

IIS Deployment: Configure the IIS server to host the application and set appropriate permissions.

Docker Container: Package your application in a container for easier deployment and scalability.

Environment Settings: Use environment variables or configuration files to set scraping parameters (e.g., target URLs, intervals).

5. Logging and Monitoring

Implement logging using libraries like Serilog or NLog to track errors and scraper performance.

Set up monitoring alerts for failures or unexpected downtime.

6. Security and Best Practices

Secure sensitive data (e.g., login credentials or API keys) using Azure Key Vault, AWS Secrets Manager, or similar tools.

Rate-limit and throttle scraping requests to avoid being blocked by the target websites.

By following this structured approach, you can deploy and automate your web scraper effectively on your ASP.NET host, ensuring it operates efficiently and reliably.

9.2 Hosting Your ASP.NET Scrapers on Azure or AWS

Web scraping applications often require robust infrastructure for reliable performance, scalability, and security. Hosting your ASP.NET scrapers on cloud platforms like Microsoft Azure or Amazon Web Services (AWS) is an excellent choice due to the array of features these platforms offer. Here's a detailed guide to hosting such applications.

Key Considerations for Hosting ASP.NET Scrapers

1. **Performance Requirements**
   Scrapers can be resource-intensive, especially when scraping large datasets or running parallel tasks. Both Azure and AWS provide scalable compute options to handle these workloads.

2. **Scalability**
   Scraping workloads might vary over time. You'll want a hosting solution that can scale up during high demand and scale down during idle times to optimize costs.

3. **Compliance and Security**
   Ensure that your scraper adheres to ethical scraping practices and complies with relevant laws and terms of service for the websites you're targeting. Use cloud features for secure data handling.

4. **Data Storage**
   Scraped data often needs storage that supports high availability, backups, and retrieval speed. Azure and AWS offer various storage options that can cater to these needs.

Hosting on Microsoft Azure

1. App Service

- **Use Case**: Ideal for smaller-scale scraping tasks.
- **Features**:
    - Fully managed platform for ASP.NET apps.
    - Auto-scaling capabilities.
    - Built-in CI/CD integration.
- **Setup**:
  Deploy your ASP.NET scraper directly from Visual Studio or a CI/CD pipeline.
  Azure App Service also supports containerized deployments if your scraper uses Docker.

2. Virtual Machines

- **Use Case**: For custom configurations or higher flexibility.

- **Features**:
    - Full control over the server environment.
    - Scalability using Azure Scale Sets.
    - Integration with Azure Monitor for logs and performance tracking.
- **Setup**:
  Deploy a Windows or Linux VM, configure IIS or Kestrel, and deploy your ASP.NET application.

3. Azure Functions

- **Use Case**: Event-driven scraping (e.g., scraping triggered by an HTTP request).
- **Features**:
    - Pay-as-you-go pricing.
    - Serverless architecture.
    - Automatic scaling for bursts of activity.
- **Setup**:
  Write your scraper as a Function App and deploy it.

Hosting on Amazon Web Services (AWS)

1. Elastic Beanstalk

- **Use Case**: Managed hosting with minimal configuration.
- **Features**:
    - Supports ASP.NET Core out of the box.
    - Auto-scaling and monitoring included.
    - Simplifies deployment and environment management.
- **Setup**:
  Deploy your app using the Elastic Beanstalk CLI or AWS Management Console.

2. EC2 (Elastic Compute Cloud)

- **Use Case**: Full control over the server.
- **Features**:
    - Wide range of instance types for different workloads.
    - Option to use Spot Instances for cost savings.
    - Integrate with CloudWatch for monitoring.

- **Setup**:
  Launch a Windows Server or Amazon Linux instance, install the necessary ASP.NET runtime, and deploy your scraper.

3. AWS Lambda

- **Use Case**: Serverless architecture for lightweight scrapers.
- **Features**:
  - Scalability and pay-per-execution pricing.
  - Integrates with other AWS services for data storage and notifications.
- **Setup**:
  Package your scraper as a Lambda function and trigger it via API Gateway, S3 events, or scheduled CloudWatch events.

Cost Optimization

Both Azure and AWS offer free tiers and flexible pricing models to help you manage costs effectively. For instance, use:

- Reserved instances or savings plans for predictable workloads.
- Auto-scaling to handle peak loads without overcommitting resources.

Monitoring and Maintenance

Set up monitoring tools:

- **Azure**: Use Azure Monitor and Application Insights for tracking performance and diagnosing issues.
- **AWS**: Use CloudWatch for logs, metrics, and alarms.

Regularly update your scraper to handle changes in target websites and optimize your scraping logic to avoid unnecessary bandwidth or compute usage.

Choosing Between Azure and AWS

Both platforms are powerful and feature-rich. Your choice may depend on:

- **Existing Ecosystem**: Azure integrates seamlessly with Microsoft products. AWS offers a broader range of services.
- **Pricing**: Compare costs based on your specific usage pattern.
- **Skill Set**: Leverage the platform you or your team are more familiar with.

By hosting your ASP.NET scrapers on Azure or AWS, you gain access to scalable, reliable, and secure environments that can support your data-gathering needs efficiently.

Development process for Azure

"With the cloud, individuals and small businesses can snap their fingers and instantly set up enterprise-class services."
- Roy Stephan

Vision

Develop well-designed ASP .NET Core applications the way you like, using Visual Studio or the dotnet CLI and Visual Studio Code or your editor of choice.

Development environment for ASP.NET Core apps

Development tools choices: IDE or editor

Whether you prefer a full and powerful IDE or a lightweight and agile editor, Microsoft has you covered when developing ASP.NET Core applications.

Visual Studio 2022. Visual Studio 2022 is the best-in-class IDE for developing applications for ASP.NET Core. It offers a host of features that increase developer productivity. You can use it to develop the application, then analyze its performance and other characteristics. The integrated debugger lets you pause code execution and step back and forth through code on the fly as it's running. Its support for hot reloads allows you to continue working with your app where you left off, even after making code changes, without having to restart the app. The built-in test runner lets you organize your tests and their results and can even perform live unit testing while you're coding. Using Live Share, you can collaborate in real-time with other developers, sharing your code session seamlessly over the network. And when you're ready, Visual Studio includes everything you need to publish your application to Azure or wherever you might host it.
Download Visual Studio 2022

Visual Studio Code and dotnet CLI (Cross-Platform Tools for Mac, Linux, and Windows). If you prefer a lightweight and cross-platform editor supporting any development language, you can use Microsoft

Visual Studio Code and the dotnet CLI. These products provide a simple yet robust experience that streamlines the developer workflow. Additionally, Visual Studio Code supports extensions for C# and web development, providing intellisense and shortcut-tasks within the editor.

Download the .NET SDK

Download Visual Studio Code

Development workflow for Azure-hosted ASP.NET Core apps

The application development lifecycle starts from each developer's machine, coding the app using their preferred language and testing it locally. Developers may choose their preferred source control system and can configure Continuous Integration (CI) and/or Continuous Delivery/Deployment (CD) using a build server or based on built-in Azure features.

To get started with developing an ASP.NET Core application using CI/CD, you can use Azure DevOps Services or your organization's own Team Foundation Server (TFS). GitHub Actions provide another option for easily building and deploying apps to Azure, for apps whose code is hosted on GitHub.

Initial setup

To create a release pipeline for your app, you need to have your application code in source control. Set up a local repository and connect it to a remote repository in a team project. Follow these instructions:

- Share your code with Git and Visual Studio or

- Share your code with TFVC and Visual Studio

Create an Azure App Service where you'll deploy your application. Create a Web App by going to the App Services blade on the Azure portal. Click +Add, select the Web App template, click Create, and provide a name and other details. The web app will be accessible from {name}.azurewebsites.net.

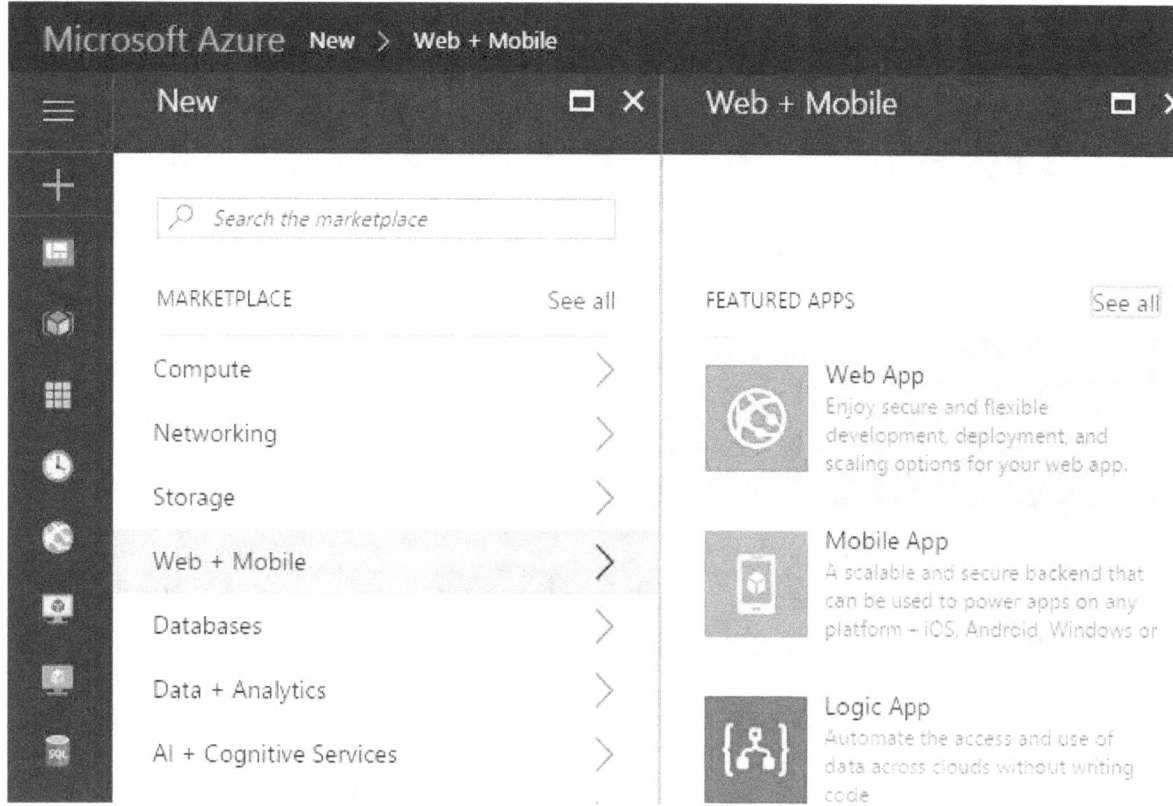

Figure 10-1. Creating a new Azure App Service Web App in the Azure Portal.

Your CI build process will perform an automated build whenever new code is committed to the project's source control repository. This process gives you immediate feedback that the code builds (and, ideally, passes automated tests) and can potentially be deployed. This CI build will produce a web deploy package artifact and publish it for consumption by your CD process.

Define your CI build process

Be sure to enable continuous integration so the system will queue a build whenever someone on your team commits new code. Test the build and verify that it is producing a web deploy package as one of its artifacts.

When a build succeeds, your CD process will deploy the results of your CI build to your Azure web app. To configure this step, you create and configure a *Release*, which will deploy to your Azure App Service.

Deploy an Azure web app

Once your CI/CD pipeline is configured, you can easily make updates to your web app and commit them to source control to have them deployed.

Workflow for developing Azure-hosted ASP.NET Core applications

Once you have configured your Azure account and your CI/CD process, developing Azure-hosted ASP.NET Core applications is simple. The following are the basic steps you usually take when building an ASP.NET Core app, hosted in Azure App Service as a Web App, as illustrated in Figure 10-2.

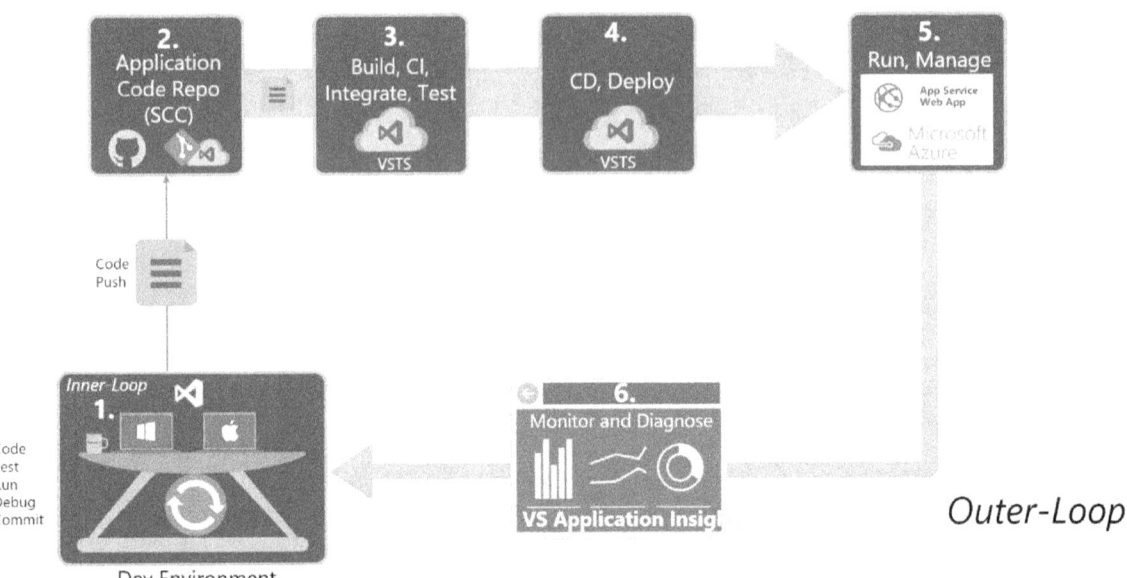

Figure 10-2. Step-by-step workflow for building ASP.NET Core apps and hosting them in Azure

Step 1. Local dev environment inner loop

Developing your ASP.NET Core application for deployment to Azure is no different from developing your application otherwise. Use the local development environment you're comfortable with, whether that's Visual Studio 2019 or the dotnet CLI and Visual Studio Code or your preferred editor. You can write code, run and debug your changes, run automated tests, and make local commits to source control until you're ready to push your changes to your shared source control repository.

Step 2. Application code repository

Whenever you're ready to share your code with your team, you should push your changes from your local source repository to your team's shared source repository. If you've been working in a custom branch, this step usually involves merging your code into a shared branch (perhaps by means of a pull request).

Step 3. Build Server: Continuous integration. build, test, package

A new build is triggered on the build server whenever a new commit is made to the shared application code repository. As part of the CI process, this build should fully compile the application and run automated tests to confirm everything is working as expected. The end result of the CI process should be a packaged version of the web app, ready for deployment.

Step 4. Build Server: Continuous delivery

Once a build has succeeded, the CD process will pick up the build artifacts produced. This process will include a web deploy package. The build server will deploy this package to Azure App Service, replacing any existing service with the newly created one. Typically this step targets a staging environment, but some applications deploy directly to production through a CD process.

Step 5. Azure App Service Web App

Once deployed, the ASP.NET Core application runs within the context of an Azure App Service Web App. This Web App can be monitored and further configured using the Azure Portal.

Step 6. Production monitoring and diagnostics

While the Web App is running, you can monitor the health of the application and collect diagnostics and user behavior data. Application Insights is included in Visual Studio, and offers automatic instrumentation for ASP.NET apps. It can provide you with information on usage, exceptions, requests, performance, and logs.

References
Build and Deploy Your ASP.NET Core App to Azure https://learn.microsoft.com/azure/devops/build-release/apps/aspnet/build-aspnet-core

Chapter 10. Azure hosting recommendations for ASP.NET Core web apps

"Line-of-business leaders everywhere are bypassing IT departments to get applications from the cloud (also known as SaaS) and paying for them like they would a magazine subscription. And when the service is no longer required, they can cancel the subscription with no equipment left unused in the corner."
- *Daryl Plummer, Gartner analyst*

Whatever your application's needs and architecture, Microsoft Azure can support it. Your hosting needs can be as simple as a static website or a sophisticated application made up of dozens of services. For ASP.NET Core monolithic web applications and supporting services, there are several well-known configurations that are recommended. The recommendations on this article are grouped based on the kind of resource to be hosted, whether full applications, individual processes, or data.

Web applications

Web applications can be hosted with:

- App Service Web Apps
- Containers (several options)
- Virtual Machines (VMs)

Of these, App Service Web Apps is the recommended approach for most scenarios, including simple container-based apps. For microservice architectures, consider a container-based approach. If you need more control over the machines running your application, consider Azure Virtual Machines.

App Service Web Apps
App Service Web Apps offers a fully managed platform optimized for hosting web applications. It's a

platform as a service (PaaS) offering that lets you focus on your business logic, while Azure takes care of the infrastructure needed to run and scale the app. Some key features of App Service Web Apps:

CHAPTER 10 | Azure hosting recommendations for ASP.NET Core web apps

- DevOps optimization (continuous integration and delivery, multiple environments, A/B testing, scripting support).
- Global scale and high availability.
- Connections to SaaS platforms and your on-premises data.
- Security and compliance.

- Visual Studio integration.

Azure App Service is the best choice for most web apps. Deployment and management are integrated into the platform, sites can scale quickly to handle high traffic loads, and the built-in load balancing and traffic manager provide high availability. You can move existing sites to Azure App Service easily with an online migration tool. You can use an open-source app from the Web Application Gallery, or create a new site using the framework and tools of your choice. The WebJobs feature makes it easy to add background job processing to your App Service web app. If you have an existing ASP.NET application hosted on-premises using a local database, there's a clear path to migrate. You can use App Service Web App with an Azure SQL Database (or secure access to your on-premises database server, if preferred).

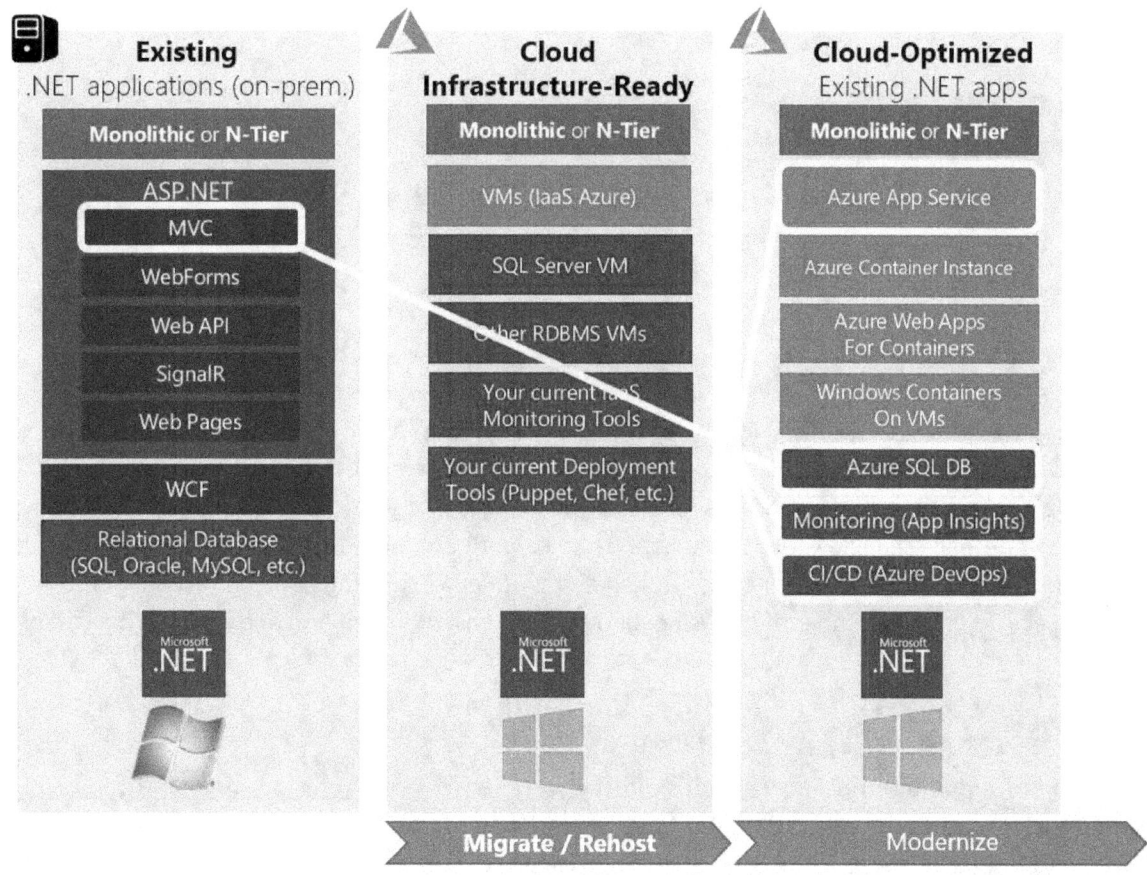

In most cases, moving from a locally hosted ASP.NET app to an App Service Web App is a straightforward process. Little or no modification should be required of the app itself, and it can quickly start to take advantage of the many features that Azure App Service Web Apps offer.

In addition to apps that are not optimized for the cloud, Azure App Service Web Apps are an excellent solution for many simple monolithic (non-distributed) applications, such as many ASP.NET Core apps. In this approach, the architecture is basic and simple to understand and manage:

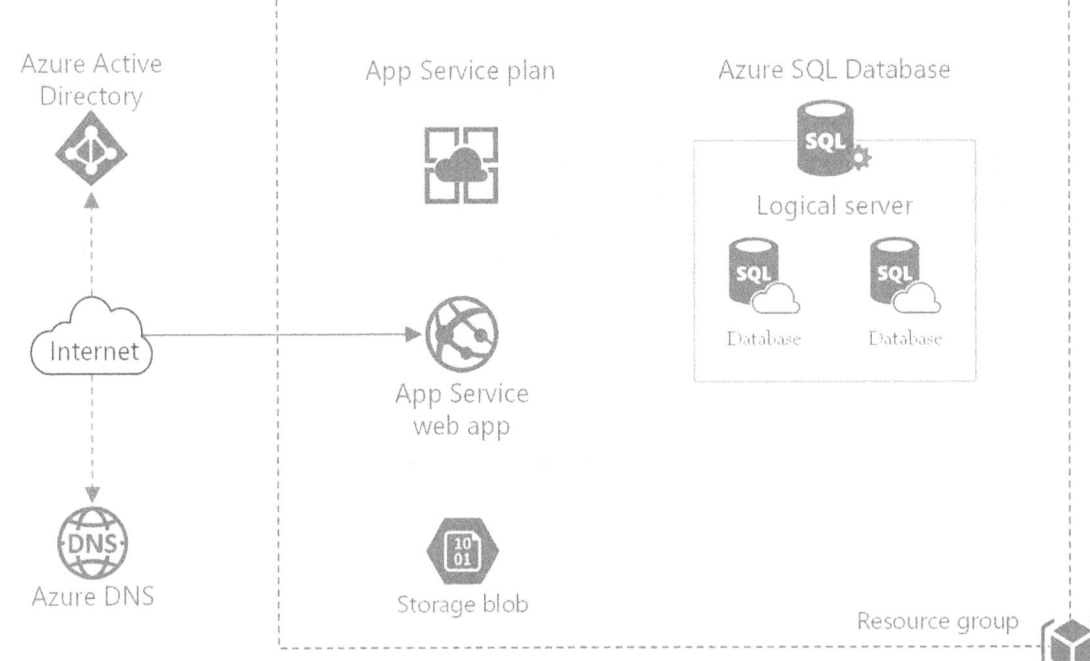

A small number of resources in a single resource group is typically sufficient to manage such an app. Apps that are typically deployed as a single unit, rather than those apps that are made up of many separate processes, are good candidates for this basic architectural approach. Though architecturally simple, this approach still allows the hosted app to scale both up (more resources per node) and out (more hosted nodes) to meet any increase in demand. With autoscale, the app can be configured to automatically adjust the number of nodes hosting the app based on demand and average load across nodes.

App Service Web Apps for Containers

In addition to support for hosting web apps directly, App Service Web Apps for Containers can be used to run containerized applications on Windows and Linux. Using this service, you can easily deploy and run containerized applications that can scale with your business. The apps have all of the features of App Service Web Apps listed above. In addition, Web Apps for Containers supports streamlined CI/CD with Docker Hub, Azure Container Registry, and GitHub. You can use Azure DevOps

to define build and deployment pipelines that publish changes to a registry. These changes can then be tested in a staging environment and automatically deployed to production using deployment slots, allowing zero-downtime upgrades. Rolling back to previous versions can be done just as easily.
There are a few scenarios where Web Apps for Containers makes the most sense. If you have existing apps that you can containerize, whether in Windows or Linux containers, you can host these easily using this toolset. Just publish your container and then configure Web Apps for Containers to pull the latest version of that image from your registry of choice. This is a "lift and shift" approach to migrating from classic app hosting models to a cloud-optimized model.

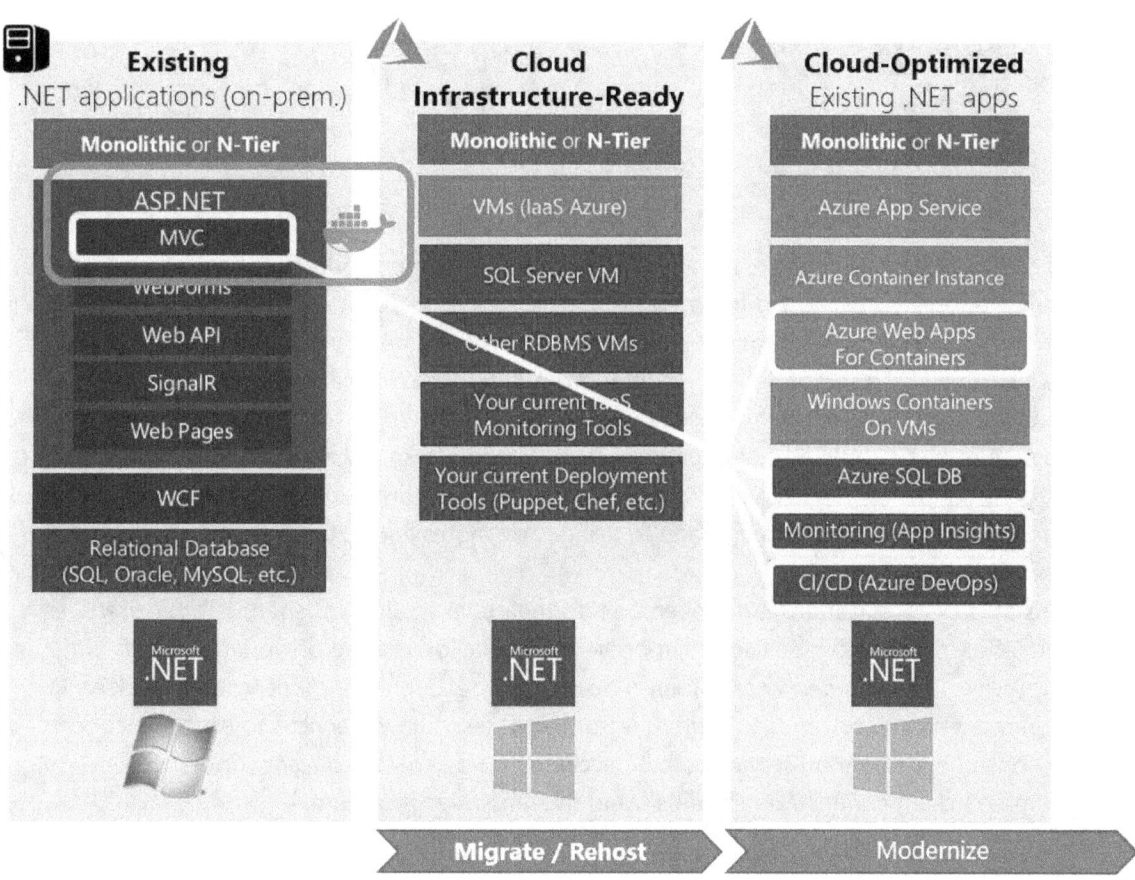

This approach also works well if your development team is able to move to a container-based development process. The "inner loop" of developing apps with containers includes building the app with containers. Changes made to the code as well as to container configuration are pushed to source control, and an automated build is responsible for publishing new container images to a registry like Docker Hub or Azure Container Registry. These images are then used as the basis for additional development, as well as for deployments to production, as shown in the following diagram:

End to End Docker DevOps Lifecycle Workflow

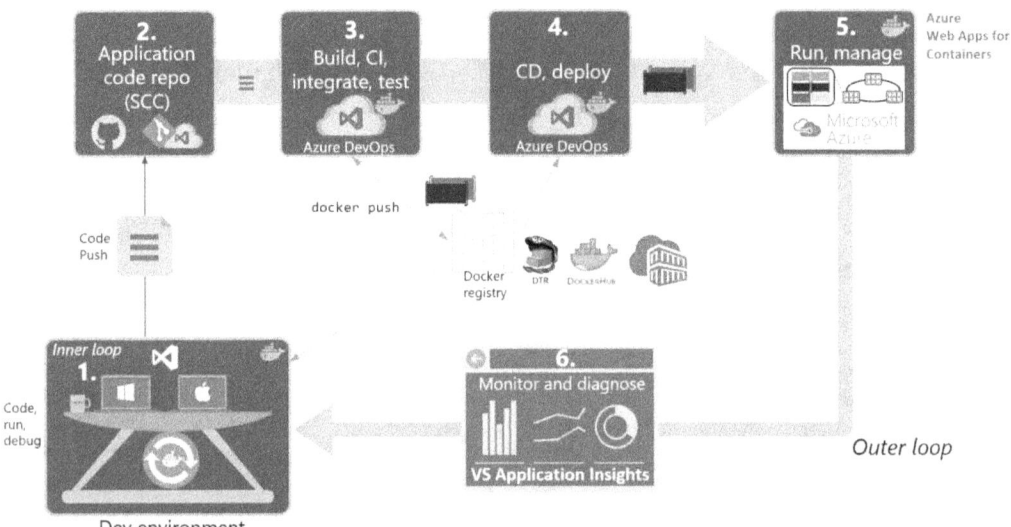

Developing with containers offers many advantages, especially when containers are used in production. The same container configuration is used to host the app in each environment in which it runs, from the local development machine to build and test systems to production. This approach greatly reduces the likelihood of defects resulting from differences in machine configuration or software versions. Developers can also use whatever tools they're most productive with, including the operating system, since containers can run on any OS. In some cases, distributed applications involving many containers may be very resource-intensive to run on a single development machine. In this scenario, it may make sense to upgrade to using Kubernetes and Azure Dev Spaces, covered in the next section.

As portions of larger applications are broken up into their own smaller, independent *microservices*, additional design patterns can be used to improve app behavior. Instead of working directly with individual services, an *API gateway* can simplify access and decouple the client from its back end. Having separate service back ends for different front ends also allows services to evolve in concert with their consumers. Common services can be accessed via a separate *sidecar* container, which might include common client connectivity libraries using the *ambassador* pattern.

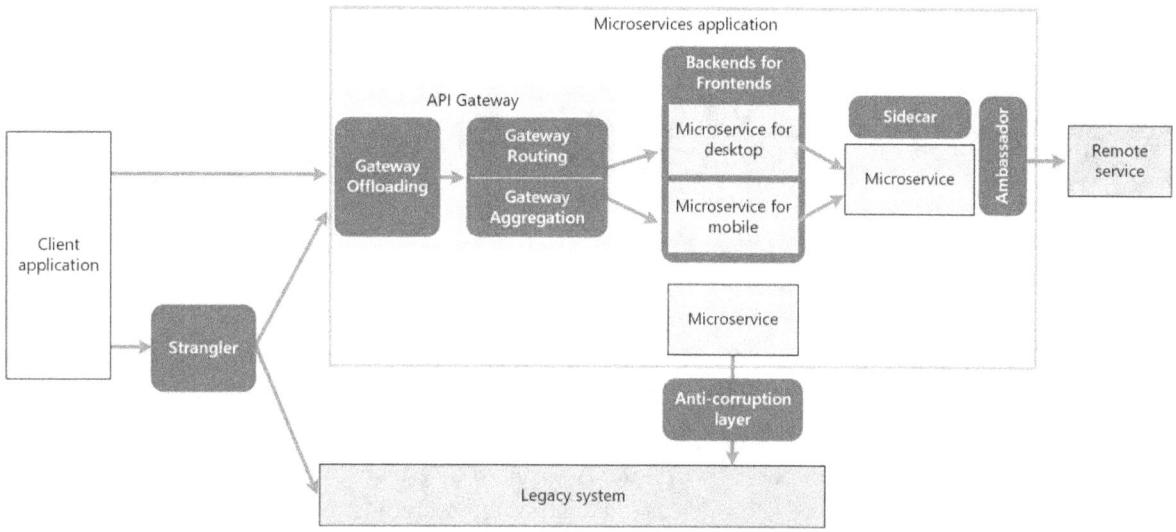

Learn more about design patterns to consider when building microservice-based systems.

Azure Kubernetes Service

Azure Kubernetes Service (AKS) manages your hosted Kubernetes environment, making it quick and easy to deploy and manage containerized applications without container orchestration expertise. It also eliminates the burden of ongoing operations and maintenance by provisioning, upgrading, and scaling resources on-demand, without taking your applications offline.

AKS reduces the complexity and operational overhead of managing a Kubernetes cluster by offloading much of that responsibility to Azure. As a hosted Kubernetes service, Azure handles critical tasks like health monitoring and maintenance for you. Also, you pay only for the agent nodes within your clusters, not for the masters. As a managed Kubernetes service, AKS provides:

- Automated Kubernetes version upgrades and patching.
- Easy cluster scaling.
- Self-healing hosted control plane (masters).
- Cost savings - pay only for running agent pool nodes.

With Azure handling the management of the nodes in your AKS cluster, you no longer need to perform many tasks manually, like cluster upgrades. Because Azure handles these critical maintenance tasks for you, AKS doesn't provide direct access (such as with SSH) to the cluster.

Teams who are leveraging AKS can also take advantage of Azure Dev Spaces. Azure Dev Spaces helps teams to focus on the development and rapid iteration of their microservice application by allowing teams to work directly with their entire microservices architecture or application running in AKS. Azure Dev Spaces also provides a way to independently update portions of your microservices architecture in isolation without affecting the rest of the AKS cluster or other developers.

CHAPTER 10 | Azure hosting recommendations for ASP.NET Core web apps

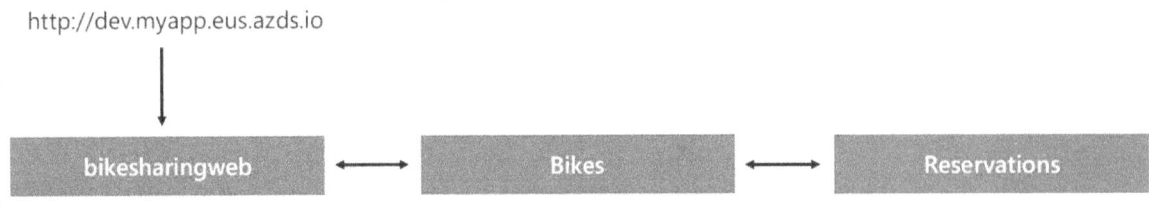

Azure Dev Spaces:
- Minimize local machine setup time and resource requirements
- Allow teams to iterate more rapidly
- Reduce the number of integration environments required by a team
- Remove the need to mock certain services in a distributed system when developing/testing

Learn more about Azure Dev Spaces

Azure Virtual Machines

If you have an existing application that would require substantial modifications to run in App Service, you could choose Virtual Machines in order to simplify migrating to the cloud. However, correctly configuring, securing, and maintaining VMs requires much more time and IT expertise compared to Azure App Service. If you're considering Azure Virtual Machines, make sure you take into account the ongoing maintenance effort required to patch, update, and manage your VM environment. Azure Virtual Machines is infrastructure as a service (IaaS), while App Service is PaaS. You should also consider whether deploying your app as a Windows Container to Web App for Containers might be a viable option for your scenario.

Logical processes

Individual logical processes that can be decoupled from the rest of the application may be deployed independently to Azure Functions in a "serverless" manner. Azure Functions lets you just write the code you need for a given problem, without worrying about the application or infrastructure to run it. You can choose from a variety of programming languages, including C#, F#, Node.js, Python, and PHP, allowing you to pick the most productive language for the task at hand. Like most cloud-based solutions, you pay only for the amount of time your use, and you can trust Azure Functions to scale up as needed.

Data

Azure offers a wide variety of data storage options, so that your application can use the appropriate data provider for the data in question.

For transactional, relational data, Azure SQL Databases are the best option. For high performance read-mostly data, a Redis cache backed by an Azure SQL Database is a good solution.

Unstructured JSON data can be stored in a variety of ways, from SQL Database columns to Blobs or Tables in Azure Storage, to Azure Cosmos DB. Of these, Azure Cosmos DB offers the best querying functionality, and is the recommended option for large numbers of JSON-based documents that must support querying.

Transient command- or event-based data used to orchestrate application behavior can use Azure Service Bus or Azure Storage Queues. Azure Service Bus offers more flexibility and is the recommended service for non-trivial messaging within and between applications.

Architecture recommendations

Your application's requirements should dictate its architecture. There are many different Azure services available. Choosing the right one is an important decision. Microsoft offers a gallery of reference architectures to help identify typical architectures optimized for common scenarios. You may find a reference architecture that maps closely to your application's requirements, or at least offers a starting point.

Figure 11-1 shows an example reference architecture. This diagram describes a recommended architecture approach for a Sitecore content management system website optimized for marketing.

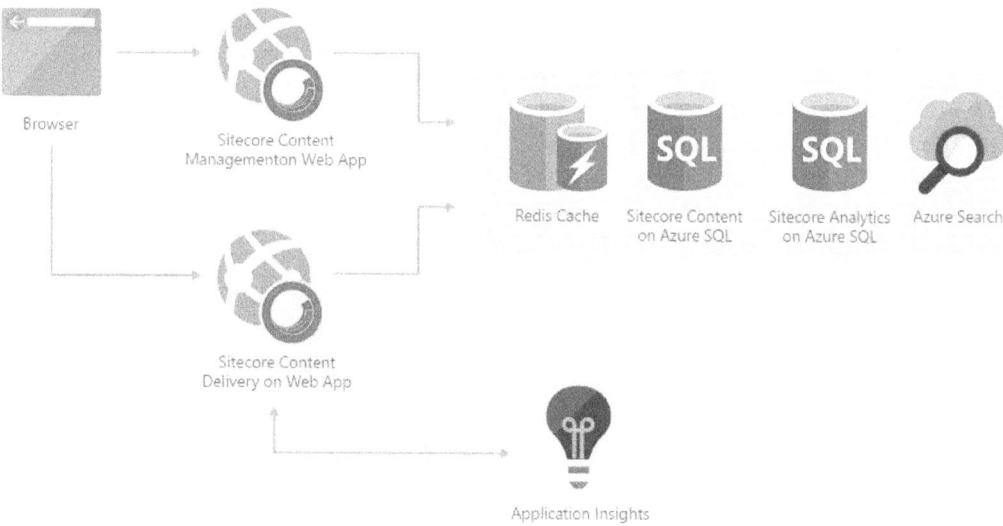

Figure 11-1. Sitecore marketing website reference architecture.

References – Azure hosting recommendations

- Azure Solution Architectures
  https://azure.microsoft.com/solutions/architecture/

- Azure Basic Web Application Architecture https://learn.microsoft.com/azure/architecture/reference-architectures/app-service-web-app/basic-web-app
- Design Patterns for Microservices https://learn.microsoft.com/azure/architecture/microservices/design/patterns
- Azure Developer Guide https://azure.microsoft.com/campaigns/developer-guide/

- Web Apps overview https://learn.microsoft.com/azure/app-service/app-service-web-overview

- Web App for Containers https://azure.microsoft.com/services/app-service/containers/

- Introduction to Azure Kubernetes Service (AKS) https://learn.microsoft.com/azure/aks/intro-kubernetes

www.ingramcontent.com/pod-product-compliance
Lightning Source LLC
Chambersburg PA
CBHW062218220526
45471CB00009B/3248